LET'S LIVE

RAMY NAOUSS

LET'S LIVE

Challenging yourself is the way

RAMY NAOUSS

Let's Live
Copyright © 2024 Ramy Naouss
First published in 2024

Print: 978-1-76124-175-8
E-book: 978-1-76124-177-2
Hardback: 978-1-76124-176-5

All rights reserved. No part of this book may be reproduced, stored in a retrieval system, or transmitted by any means (electronic, mechanical, photocopying, recording, or otherwise) without written permission from the author.

Because of the dynamic nature of the Internet, any web addresses or links contained in this book may have changed since publication and may no longer be valid. The information in this book is based on the author's experiences and opinions. The views expressed in this book are solely those of the author and do not necessarily reflect the views of the publisher; the publisher hereby disclaims any responsibility for them.

The author of this book does not dispense any form of medical, legal, financial, or technical advice either directly or indirectly. The intent of the author is solely to provide information of a general nature to help you in your quest for personal development and growth. In the event you use any of the information in this book, the author and the publisher assume no responsibility for your actions. If any form of expert assistance is required, the services of a competent professional should be sought.

Publishing information
Publishing and design facilitated by Passionpreneur Publishing
A division of Passionpreneur Organization Pty Ltd
ABN: 48640637529

Melbourne, VIC | Australia
www.passionpreneurpublishing.com

*This book is dedicated to my auntie,
who passed away from cancer in March 2023.
I achieved my first world record for her,
and her approach to life and
death has touched me deeply.*

*She was the happiest person I ever met;
even in her final days, she was always smiling.
She kept saying, "Love life".*

*I'm sharing her message—actually,
the only true message out there—love.*

TABLE OF CONTENTS

Dedication	v
Acknowledgments	ix
Introduction	1
Uncertainty is the Only Certainty in Life	5
We are Born to Run	11

PART 1: AS WE RUN, WE BECOME	17
Run for Your Life	19
The Secret of Winning Your Mornings	27
All You Need is One Good Decision	31

PART 2: NEW BEGINNINGS, BETTER THINGS	37
New Beginnings, Better Things	39
One Moment Can Change Your Life	47
Devil's Day	59

PART 3: PATH TO SERENDIPITY	63
Life Happens Outside Our Minds	65
Art of Curiosity	75

PART 4: A NEW START AND MANY POSSIBILITIES	81
New Year, New Me	83

PART 5: FIND STRENGTH IN PAIN — 91
Pain is the Way — 93

PART 6: WHAT YOU ARE SEEKING IS SEEKING YOU — 105
All the Answers are Within — 107

PART 7: ACCEPTANCE IS THE KEY — 113
Accept What Life Has to Offer — 115
All Set and Done — 123
Your Life Is in Your Hands — 129
Time to Harvest the Fruits — 137

PART 8: SLOWLY BUT SURELY — 145
New Era — 147
4 Whys — 155

PART 9: LIVE LIFE — 165
How Would You Know if You Don't Try? — 167
Outwitting the Devil — 175
I Watched My Own Funeral — 191
There is No Reality — 197
Let's Live — 205

Conclusion — 209
Author Bio — 213
Blurb — 215

ACKNOWLEDGMENTS

I'm forever grateful to Mom and Dad for bringing me into this life, raising me the best they could, and teaching me the most ethical values, and to my sister, who has always supported me throughout every step. I'm blessed for the people in my life—Zaher, Jhony, Dima and Joe, and my cousins, Isabella, Anna, Bahre, Rawad, Ashraf, and Ryan.

I'm also grateful to each person who reacted to my videos, came to an event, and believed in life's beauty. I love each and every one of them.

Do good, and good will come to you. Life has always treated me well, even when it was hard, and I am fully aware it is because of people's intentions.

INTRODUCTION

You and I, since we were kids, have been searching for a feeling. When we were kids, we stayed next to our parents (to feel safe), hugged our friends in kindergarten (to feel love), and ate chocolate (to feel pleasure). The examples are many.

But as we get older, those same feelings become harder to attain. Feeling safe isn't staying next to our parents anymore, and hugging our friends makes us skeptical about what they'll think about us.

It's safe to say that the feelings we grew up searching for become masked by judgment, overthinking, low self-esteem, and fear.

It all boils down to one reason: When we become teenagers, there was a voice inside our heads, which I refer to as "the devil" throughout this book. This voice steals those feelings, the purity, the simplicity, and the feeling of being alive from us.

Actually, the devil doesn't steal our feelings but holds us back and causes us to miss out on life until we reclaim them—and it's challenging to do so. We can calm this voice down through alcohol, drugs, pills, and so on.

If we love our friend, we wait until both of us get drunk to tell them, "I love you!" When we love a girl, we wait until both of us are high to express our love for her, when the devil is numb, and all the barriers are low. However, the side effects are disastrous—both physically and mentally—and the reality becomes delusional.

Me, you, him, her, us—we're all the same. I was always searching for those feelings, doing whatever I could to feed my ego. It made me feel good but ignorant of my surroundings. Drinking alcohol made me feel confident, but I felt bad the next day and realized that the confidence I had the previous night was fake. In the same way, smoking a joint made me feel good, loose, and able to laugh; I felt lazy and crashed until the next hit.

All those feelings were an instant dopamine hit that disappeared just as quickly.

Years later, I discovered the feeling I was always searching for—the feeling I believe all of us are searching for—the feeling beyond instant pleasure, beyond a high, and beyond any physicality.

I achieved that feeling through running barefoot, reading, meditating, and challenging myself. When I felt it once, there was no going back. My life was never the same.

This book isn't a motivational book telling you, "You can do it", "Stand up", "Go run". I call such nonsense "mental orgasms". This book is NOT about the action of running as a workout; in fact, you should neither work out the way that I do, nor challenge yourself the same way that I did.

In this book, I'm sharing a new dimension of living I discovered by chance. Running was the first thing that helped me tap into it, which I pushed later by challenging myself with other elements, such as breathing and meditation. These were the keys to reaching this ultimate feeling that I call "bliss", which I never knew existed.

After making a constant effort for a long time, it eventually all made sense.

Keep in mind the fact that I hated running. I had knee and back pain, and I was a very lazy person. My life was a combination of late-night parties, oversleeping, procrastination, seeking instant gratification, and so on. I never really put much effort into the various aspects of my life. I always hoped to achieve my dreams, but never really worked for them.

Until I got diagnosed with blood cancer in 2017, which was my first reality check. These so-called reality checks kept coming, and I called them "hits".

After three years of recovering from my cancer, I was *hit* for the second time. This time, I was broke and deep in debt.

With nothing to lose and a hunger to step up, I began my quest to become better and making a little effort by running, reading, meditating, and challenging myself.

Life changed. For the better.

At the time of writing this book, I've run over 1,100 kilometers in six months, including four marathons and two ultramarathons—all barefoot. I'll share more on this later in the book.

I currently hold the Guinness World Record for standing on nail boards for twelve hours, twelve minutes, and eight seconds.

I have founded my own business, where I help individuals from around the world tap into their potential mentally, physically, and spiritually. I carried out hundreds of events dealing with thousands of people, starting in the United Arab Emirates and Lebanon, and eventually spreading around the globe.

However, this book isn't about those achievements—it's about the peace, clarity, and quality of life I'm living and feeling from within.

This book is a way to share all of it with you.

Let's go, baby!

UNCERTAINTY IS THE ONLY CERTAINTY IN LIFE

"We are born twice, once into existence and the second into life."

January 7, 2017

I wake up sick. I've been under the weather, on and off, for the past month. It's winter in Lebanon, and I'm telling myself that it could just be a cold or the flu. I'm wondering why I'm not getting better, though. I've taken one round of antibiotics already.

I walk to the living room. Mom is on the couch drinking her tea, and I tell her, "Mom, I think I'm not fine." She asks, "Do you have a fever?" I reply, "I've been sweating all night. I think there probably is. I feel cold."

While we're speaking, I cough. I reach out for a tissue and then another cough—a deep one. I look at the tissue and see blood.

Mom reaches for her phone and calls her brother. My uncle is a cardiologist—he's both family and the family doctor.

Mom says into the phone, "Ramy coughed up blood."

Uncle replies, "Come to the hospital. I'll meet you in ten."

You know that feeling when you know something is wrong but are in denial, insisting that you're fine? I felt this, but I love and trust my uncle, so hospital it was.

I enter the emergency room and describe my symptoms to the doctors and nurses. They conduct a blood test and perform a chest X-ray.

In no time, my uncle is with me again in the hospital, asking if I'd mind having another blood test. I agree.

Ten minutes later, my uncle returns and says, "I think the nurse didn't withdraw enough blood. Just one more time."

I reply, "Sure, *Khalo*." Khalo means uncle in Arabic.

Another ten minutes go by, and my uncle mentions that I have bronchitis, which is why I coughed up blood. He adds, "It's better for you to stay in the hospital and take the meds through IV. It's better for your recovery."

So, I stay in the hospital, but I'm frustrated. I'd booked a table at Sky Bar. I wanted to party.

Life is unfair sometimes. That's what I thought.

January 8, 2017

It's a Sunday. After spending a boring night in the hospital counting the seconds, I'm happy that I can leave the next day.

My uncle calls Mom, Dad, and my sister. They all gather around my bed in the hospital. My uncle then says, "There is bad and worse news. We all wish not to face either, but this isn't what happens in life."

I wonder what he's talking about. I'm eager to leave the hospital and enjoy my weekend.

He continues, "I spoke with my colleague yesterday and assessed the case. We've prepared the treatment for you."

What treatment? I wonder. The words he's saying aren't making sense. I'm confused and not feeling good.

My uncle says, "Usually, the white blood cell count should be a maximum of 10,000 per microliter. Your white blood cells are 210,000 per microliter."

While he's speaking, I'm thinking: *This is not very good.*

My uncle says, "You've been diagnosed with chronic myeloid leukemia, a type of blood cancer. But don't …" All I hear after the word "cancer" is noise. I didn't really process any words that came after.

I'm hoping that it's one of those nightmares, and I'll wake up shortly. But it seems this is real. I'm not waking up. I turn to my left. Mom isn't moving. I turn to my right. My sister is barely breathing. I look at Dad. He's listening attentively with no reaction. I want this to end. As soon as possible. But it doesn't. I hear my uncle finally stop talking.

Life is mellow at this moment. I think I'm delusional. I'm not sure what is reality and what isn't. I start shaking. Mom is crying. My sister is hugging me with tears in her eyes.

Dad says, "It's going to be all right, Son."

You know how when a baby is born, he cries nonstop? The mother holds him in her arms. I'm back in this state. I'm crying, with my face between Mom's palms, asking, "Mom, am I going to die? I don't want to die."

Mom replies through tears, "I'd be next to you, *habibi*. I won't leave you. We're going to get through this."

I'm in a hospital, crying. All my family and friends come by to visit me. Doctors are continuously checking on me. I ask everyone to leave me alone. For some time.

I'm in my bed, drowning in tears, absorbing the shock. My thoughts are continuous questions: *Why me? What did I do wrong?*

Sometime later that day, I say, "F**k it. I'm going to get over it. Why not?"

Little did I know, I was being born again. It was exactly what had happened when I was actually born. Once again, I'm crying on Mom's lap in a hospital, staying in isolation for a while, and all the family is gathered around me. Only this time, it was twenty-five years later.

I spent the first twenty-four hours reading, researching, and asking people about my case.

What doctors believe is based on statistics and numbers. Studies show that out of one hundred people, only seventy percent benefit from treatments. Thirty percent don't.

However, statistics and science only work when dealing with large numbers because if you study only one individual, those statistics don't mean much.

You can't recover to seventy percent and still be thirty percent not recovered. This is why, in my personal opinion, I believe numbers and science aren't the only way. We've barely discovered and understood ten percent (if I'm being generous) of everything there is to know about life.

That day, I promised myself I'd do whatever it took to recover. I researched, studied, and experimented. I believed my body had a problem for a reason and that understanding that reason would allow me to help my body reverse the illness.

What I knew previously about life ... I stopped believing it, wanting to go back to zero so I could study and learn about life in depth. I decided that I wasn't going to believe anyone, because if I was diagnosed with cancer for no reason (science always approaches cancer as having no specific reason for its presence), then there was no reason for me not to create my life in the way I desired.

I decided I'd do whatever it took to gain back my health and reclaim what was stolen from me. Life.

Let me take you on my journey of how I regained my life.

It's going to be a good one, baby! Let's go.

WE ARE BORN TO RUN

"But we learn how to walk."

Before deliveries, supermarkets, cars, buildings and all the privileged options we have nowadays, humans had to run for water, food, and shelter, as well as to explore and expand.

Yet the world we live in today, with all its advantages, has made us lazy. With a click of a button on my phone, I can order food, groceries, furniture, or any other service I demand. I can stay on the couch twenty-four hours a day for seven days a week and have all my desires land on my lap through a device I carry in my hand.

It sounds convenient, but this has a tremendously negative effect on our wellbeing. Becoming lazy leads to the body and mind having nothing to fight for, so they start fighting themselves. The body begins creating diseases within, and the mind creates stress, anxiety, depression, and so on.

The latest studies in the last five years show that diabetes, cholesterol, depression, cancer, anxiety, obesity, and mental illnesses are on the rise at a pace that we've never witnessed in the history of humanity.

- Diabetes: The International Diabetes Federation stated that five hundred million people worldwide have diabetes. That amounts to around 14 percent of the world's population.
- Cholesterol: The World Heart Federation stated that 39 percent of the world's population is affected by cholesterol.
- Depression: The World Health Organization stated that 5 percent of the population worldwide is diagnosed with depression, and this number is expected to rise by 2 percent over the next few years. This equates to approximately 280 to 310 million people.
- Cancer: World Cancer Research Funds stated that 5.5 percent of the worldwide population has been diagnosed with a certain type of cancer.

If you look more deeply into that prognosis and you have minimal knowledge about health and the mind–body connection, here are a few facts to add:

- Diabetes and cholesterol, in 90 percent of cases, can be cured just by moving the body and breathing.
- Depression can be reduced by 70–75 percent with body movement, meditation, and breathing—I'll elaborate on this later.
- Cancer can be prevented by lifestyle, food, diet, fasting, movement, and thought patterns, and can be reduced by 40 percent.

Could it be that we've become extremely lazy to the point where we're blind and can't read between the lines? Maybe life became so easy that we became very weak.

As Anna Lembke mentions in her book *Dopamine Nation*, "We are pleasuring ourselves to death."

Fifty years from now, imagine your kids and grandkids have developed in such a way that their lower bodies have become weak with their spines bent forward. The simple motion of walking is hard due to a continuous lack of movement. They avoid any movement requiring effort unless they use moving chairs or other technologies that "simplify" life.

Instead of evolving, we're going backward. The immense usage of phones has been on the rise, now averaging five to seven hours daily. I believe it will rise to between eight and ten hours daily in the next few years. The effect of such exploitation of our devices will lead to curved spines and back pain, a fifty percent loss of strength in the body, and fingers crunched inward, causing our hands to lose forty percent of their efficiency.

Just look around—the gym, the airport, the beach—and you'll see it. Imagine if we stay stuck in this hypnotic rhythm. Where will we land?

Crazy, man! No!

Despite this, I'm not here to plant negative thoughts. I'm here to make you conscious of how unconscious our lives are. If we only become more aware of the problem—you, me, and our friends and family—we can change all of this. We can live healthy, happy, strong, and beautiful lives.

Remember, the hardest part of arriving at the solution is understanding the problem. No matter how fast humans are evolving, it's essential that we stop, observe, assess, and adjust.

It all starts with one person. Me. You.

You're reading this book for a reason. Perhaps it's by chance or luck, or maybe you experienced a calling to change your life.

Maybe you've been following me, and you wanted to understand why I run every day, why I constantly push myself, or why I always challenge myself and endure physical pain.

Here, I'm sharing my deepest thoughts with you. Always remember that if what I'm saying resonates with you, we're one step forward, brother and sister, to a better you, a better me, a better world, and a better life. We can reverse those bad statistics and live a good life.

When I started the discovery journey after my recovery from cancer, many people shared their thoughts with me.

"Man, why are you putting in that much effort? Running, standing on nail boards, fasting for long periods?"

"Just live a normal life, bro, and when you die … you'll die anyway."

This is an absurd way to look at life. Allow me to explain why.

Do you know who was thousands of times more shocked than me when I was diagnosed with cancer? Mom, my sister, and Dad.

Imagine, they were in shock and pain and were crying for me. It took them months to understand what happened on January 8, 2017—the day I was diagnosed. It's still stuck with them.

For me, though, it took a couple of days to understand.

Life isn't just about you.

If you change, I change, and he and she grow. We improve, we stretch ourselves, we get better, and we help people around us—we evolve. Trust me. We reverse the old numbers and create better ones.

Let me share with you how I started to improve my life by running, reading, meditating, and changing my habits.

PART 1

AS WE RUN, WE BECOME

RUN FOR YOUR LIFE

"Running doesn't teach you how to become healthy,
but it teaches you how to thrive."

— Unknown

The first year after diagnosis was a rollercoaster of emotions. One day I felt good, and the next, low. Handling the treatment and constantly worrying if I was benefiting from the treatment were common thoughts for me.

I faced major issues with the treatment, which was chemotherapy pills. Until March 2017, my platelets (small, colorless cell fragments in our blood that form clots and stop or prevent bleeding) dropped to 10,000 per microliter, which was supposed to be 150,000 to 450,000 per microliter for a normal, healthy person. I was living in fear of internal bleeding if I so much as sneezed or hit my head. It was frustrating. It was worse than being in prison, but every day showed a slow improvement, medically and mentally.

By the end of 2019, my cancer situation was under control. All my test results were good; I just had to keep taking the treatment pills as a precaution for a while. I had a joyful summer of traveling, partying, and enjoying other leisure experiences. I wanted to feel normal again. I had been practicing magic for the past thirteen years, living in Dubai and performing here and there. Life was fair. I was neither broke nor rich, sad nor ecstatic, and I was surrounded by wonderful people.

Yet, since my school days, I'd been an outcast (I believe we all are, but some people hide it), dreaming of becoming an international magician and never settling for a casual life. However, my dreams and thoughts were way beyond my reality.

I took a break after the crazy summer of 2019 and reflected on my life. I wrote down my goals for 2020 and started to redesign my life, aiming to create a morning routine.

I returned to Dubai at the end of October 2019, having had enough of the previous nonsense after developing a growth mindset. I was sick of waiting for someone to help me and tired of lying to myself. I remember telling myself, "Enough is enough. It's time to walk the talk. Starting today with what I have and what I know now."

It was summer, and I usually woke up at midday. I decided this was a good place to start and began changing this bad habit by waking up slightly earlier, around 10:00 a.m. The routine was to wake up, read, meditate, and write down my goals before checking my phone. I noticed two things:

1. With this small window of serenity, my mind calmed down, and I became less agitated.
2. Being in peace for thirty minutes during the day helped me gain clarity about my future.

Unfortunately, I only did it for a few days before distractions caused me to wander off track. I was clubbing, getting drunk, meeting girls, and so on, which messed up the next few mornings. I tried to fall back into the new, good habits again, but I was stuck in the same loop—do it well for a few days, then veer off track again.

Remember, back then, my goal—the big goal—was to become an international magician. Reading, writing, and meditating were small daily practices that helped me visualize the change I wanted.

After some research and study, I realized that the internet would be the best way to become an international magician. I decided to make one video per week on my YouTube channel; one of those videos would go viral, triggering international attention.

I knew this would take time, and I had no knowledge of making or editing videos. So, I embarked on a journey of consistency, determined to stay focused and create one video every week.

This will make sense soon. Bear with me.

I started reading biographies and learning from inspirational individuals about how they were able to create their own success. I noticed that most stars, entrepreneurs, and influential people tended to be in the habit of running in the morning. I remember thinking, well, if one of the characteristics to become successful is to run, then I'll have to run.

Let me give you a glimpse of how I kicked off my running journey in January 2020. Remember how, at the start of this book, I told you that I hated running? Every time I ran, I felt my knees and back ache again. The worst part of all was waking up early.

Despite the annoyance, I adjusted my morning routine to wake up at 9:30 a.m. I ran for twenty-five minutes, walking for a minute before running for another minute. I had zero knowledge about running. I wore random shoes, just putting myself out there and moving my body. I ran while listening to podcasts because I felt that running by itself was boring. I made it a habit to run three times each week. Around 10:00 a.m., I'd shower, meditate for ten minutes, and then read and write for twenty minutes.

I was just trying my best.

There's a saying: "Insanity is doing the same things every day and expecting different results." So, if I wanted to change my life, I needed to keep changing, trying, learning, adapting, and assessing my progress along the way. I was even listening to people that stretched my mind, like Jim Rohn and Sadhguru. I learned from them and their wisdom.

Of course, it wasn't that easy in the beginning. I was surrounded by so many distractions. It was easy for me to slip. For four days,

I'd focus on running, and then there'd be a party on the Friday. I'd be *dragged* there, of course, but I'd be drinking willingly and having fun, which didn't stop until Sunday.

Then, on Monday, I'd focus again on trying to get back into the zone. This was a loop for me.

I was living in the gray zone, maintaining my focus from Monday to Thursday, which was essentially nothing more than a warm-up for the mess that was Fridays and Saturdays. My Sundays were wasted on recovering for Monday, when I'd be back at it. I wasn't fully committed to my routine, but I wasn't letting go of it, either.

It's funny how two personas lived in my head: the self that wanted to get better and the other that wanted to remain the same.

I can describe it now, but I was stuck in it back then and couldn't see my two selves. I wanted to improve, but my lifestyle and the things I used to do didn't fit.

I wanted to wake up early and run but also to party late and feel good. It was like I wanted to be better, just not wholeheartedly. However, I believe that's the only way possible: you cannot just let go of all bad habits in a day. It will be possible, but slowly.

January 2020

I promised myself that whatever happened, I'd run three days each week, read fifty pages, and create one video.

Decision. Promise. Consistency. That was my motto.

In the beginning, I couldn't see the results of being consistent. I was just trying for a while, wondering if things were going to change.

At the end of February, COVID-19 hit. Airports, roads, and restaurants were all closed. I remembered what Daksha Watts said: "If you are brave enough to look, hidden within the curse, there is a deeper blessing."

Just like that, all the distractions in my life vanished. It's often funny how life just *happens*—weekends became boring, and there was nothing to do. Instead, I focused my efforts on running and all my new habits.

This is a brief overview of my 2020. Two months of complete isolation gave me time to anchor my morning routine. After quarantine, during April and May, my runs became longer. I'd read a few books, and life started to regain its normality.

At the beginning of 2021, I ran between twenty-five and thirty minutes daily with no walking in between. Seven minutes per kilometer was a reasonably fair pace! I stayed disciplined with the ups and downs, but the cycle became three weeks of complete focus, then one week of distractions. I achieved small wins compared with the previous year because I was filming my magic, editing, and posting once a week. I grew my content-creating skills and fell in love with making videos and sharing stories. Eventually, I started filming shots of random events in the sunset. It was fun.

February 2021

My mind began to stretch. It had been a year since I started trying new things. I was running, reading, and meditating, and all those atomic habits piled up. However, as an individual, I didn't feel my major change, even though my morning routine had started to stretch as well. Instead of waking up at 9:30 a.m., I was getting up at 8:30 a.m. and then 8:00 a.m. By the end of February, I was waking up at 7:00 a.m. More alone time. More peace and focus.

THE SECRET OF WINNING YOUR MORNINGS

> "How you start the day, is how you live your day. How you live your day, is how you live your life."
>
> — Louise Hay

This is what my morning looked like. At 7:00 a.m., I'd wake up, wash my face, put on my running shoes, run four kilometers, shower, drink coffee, read a book, write, and meditate until 10:00 a.m. One rule I followed consistently was not touching my phone until 10:00 a.m.

During the first three months of 2021, I was disciplined most of the time.

Seeing celebrities like Dwayne "The Rock" Johnson and Will Smith waking up at 5:30 a.m., I convinced myself that if they could do it, I could do it. I'd spent the past year reading and listening to podcasts, feeding my mind constantly, and I was ready.

The mind is like an elastic band. Once you stretch it, it can never go back to its original size. For example, once you have run five kilometers, two kilometers becomes easy. Once you can lift twenty kilograms, ten kilograms becomes easy. Once you date someone that adds a lot of value to your life, you can't go back to dating someone that doesn't provide any value to your life. Do you see what I mean?

After finishing a decent number of books, changing my mind became easy. Easy doesn't mean it didn't require any effort; it means the belief that change was possible had become accessible to me. On top of this, I was meditating, writing in my journal, observing my life, asking myself deep questions, and connecting deep within.

I started getting up at 5:30 a.m., my morning routine became longer, and the runs became enjoyable. Watching the sunrise while everyone's asleep is calming and magical. I was vibing with life, and I had birds, nature, and plenty of music in my ears.

There is a power in the morning that just isn't there throughout the rest of the day. Morning has magic. Real magic. And this comes from someone who used to create magic for audiences. Mornings are spectacular.

When you sleep at 10:00 p.m. and wake up at 5:00 a.m., your brain releases melatonin—a hormone that's been shown to improve memory and cognitive function, fight cancer, boost immune function, and move you through the five phases of sleep.

That is why getting seven hours of sleep, from 10:00 p.m. to 5:00 a.m. or 11:00 p.m. to 6:00 p.m., makes you feel fresher and more energetic than sleeping from 2:00 a.m. to 9:00 a.m. At 2:00 a.m., you've already lost three to four hours of melatonin secretion. I suggest you read *Why We Sleep* by Mathew Walker. You'll understand exactly why we sleep.

Now you know. In the morning, there is peace. Peace on the streets. Silence. It's the only time where there is daylight and no noise.

You'll never see, feel, or touch this peace except in the morning or perhaps if you live alone in the mountains, but let's forget the mountains for now. There's a greater chance of you waking up early than being alone in the mountains!

I genuinely advise you to sleep early and wake up early. Even if you must push yourself out of bed, I promise you'll feel great, my friend.

What I was experiencing while running in the morning was a dual experience. I experienced peace, silence, and serenity, and at the same time, I became fully alert, breathing and moving my body in a trance state, all while being mindful and one hundred percent in the present.

Many of our problems today, including feeling low, are there because we're never present. We have a monkey mind, jumping between worrying about the future, stressing about what could happen, and revisiting the past, feeling guilt and regret. This dual experience taught me to switch from monkey mind to monk mind.

After finishing my run, I meditate to detach from my emotions, observe my mistakes, flaws, and problems, and gain clarity on how to solve them and improve on a personal level.

This concept is commercialized nowadays as *loving yourself*.

I returned to Lebanon in the summer from May to August 2021. Guess what? I went back to the old me. Distractions were everywhere. The summer was chaotic. I was drinking, partying, and enjoying time with people visiting from abroad. It was a total mess, and there was zero self-improvement.

And running? I almost forgot about it. I thought it was okay to take a short break, but in hindsight, I was taking a break from a future I dreamed of. I was ignorant.

By the beginning of September, it was time for a new season. My other self—the one who wanted to be better—showed up again. My mentality shifted, and I remember thinking *Okay, I had a fun summer. Now it's time to focus*. The first decision I made was to hit the road for a run. My performance was bad, thanks to overindulging in drinking and smoking. I ended up finishing my five-kilometer run, which felt like a big achievement.

ALL YOU NEED IS ONE GOOD DECISION

"Out of 100 bad decisions, you only need one good decision, and your whole life will change."

I continued with my commitment to post one video every week on my YouTube channel throughout my messy summer in Lebanon. I didn't stop or skip a single week. I wasn't putting in much effort, but I was still doing it. I was consistent.

Before 2021, I made videos with titles such as *How to Kiss Girls with Magic*, *How to Win a Date with Magic*, and *How to Impress a Girl with Magic*. They were cool and trendy, and they made me look like an Alpha—or at least that's what I thought.

After September 2021, the style of my videos started to change. I was keen to create videos unrelated to magic and more focused on positive influences on myself and others. The video titles changed, with themes like *Taking a Stranger to Skydive with Me on the Spot*,

Challenging People to Stand on Nails, *Taking a Housekeeper to the Most Luxurious Hotel*, and *Magic for the Homeless*. I was riding the wave and following my feelings.

Let's Live.

The ideology that I lived by after being diagnosed with cancer, and the very same one that I had tattooed on my neck during the summer of 2018.

The words were always on the tip of my tongue. If I wanted to have a new experience like scuba diving, and my mind was doing its best to convince me not to, I'd say to myself, "Let's Live." Then, I'd end up doing it. I'm sure those two words pushed me to become more, to do more, and to be more.

In November 2021, I returned to Dubai and moved into my new place with less distractions. I was living in a very calm area with my best friend. From day one, I returned to my running and morning routine.

Running became more enjoyable, so much so that I ran five times per week. The new area I moved to had elements of nature within the concrete jungle. There were birds, greenery, and all sorts of authentic life.

If I woke up and ran, my whole day would be productive. I'd be mentally sharp and fully focused. This is a fact. If I skipped the run, my mind would be foggy that day.

While running was a workout, it also became a dimension that I entered to face my dark side, feel myself, tune into my body, and be aware.

Every day, I woke up at 5:30 a.m. As soon as I was on the street going for my run, I'd open Instagram and post the same story daily: "Good morning. Rise and shine, baby! Today is a good day to have a great day … Woohoo!" Eventually, this phrase gained some attention, and a few followers would repeat it once they saw it, when messaging me privately, or even when posting on their own social pages.

I wasn't doing it for anyone. I made a habit of saying it because it was a mantra I was repeating every day, and I was the first to hear it while recording it. How you talk to yourself is the secret that helps you set up the intention for the day.

By April 2022, I'd spent six months fully focused and away from distractions, delving deeper into running, writing, meditating, and reading. A few of the books I read were about human history and how our lives were shaped in the past. Through reading, I was eager to understand or discover a way to make my body heal itself.

I believed that if my body had fallen into some error state, creating cancer because of external and internal negative factors, it could recover if I created a proper healing environment and fueled it with healthy food and nourishing thoughts to encourage self-healing. I was sure I could find a way to heal my back pain, too.

Throughout my research and experimentations, a friend advised me to read *Born to Run* by Christopher McDougall. It's such a good book. In it, Christopher talks about how humans had to run long distances to hunt and how we used to run barefoot before all of the technological advances with shoes and cushioned soles. He goes on a journey to find a tribe called *Tarahumara*, a Mexican group that runs barefoot. It blew my mind. Christopher was completely right. Before all those innovations, barefoot was the only way of doing it.

The next day, I put on my shoes and went to the nearest park. Then, I took them off and ran barefoot for one kilometer. That day, I got home mesmerized, feeling a new high.

The day after, I left my shoes in the closet and went for an easy three-kilometer run. Completely barefoot.

Do you remember the promise I made to myself about posting one video a week on YouTube? Well, I was still doing exactly that. In two years, I hadn't skipped a single week. That is *consistency*. I kept doing it, regardless of whether I got one, ten, or a hundred views. I wasn't really getting any more than that.

I mentioned earlier that my YouTube channel was taking a different direction, and these videos are still on my channel: *@ramynaouss*. You can check them out, but the channel is now more about the theme of *Let's Live*. I didn't know what the exact purpose of it was. All I knew was that I loved life, and I wanted to explore life and share it online.

On January 8, 2022, I made a video about my cancer called *Hey Life, I Have Something to Tell You*. It's still on my YouTube channel if you want to watch it.

My skills with filming and editing were improving drastically. My best friend, Jhony, a professional filmmaker, was also helping me. Storytelling, filming, experiencing, and documenting became a new passion, and my professional job as a magician drifted away slowly. How was this happening? The dream I had been pursuing most of my life was slowly disappearing.

PART 2

NEW BEGINNINGS, BETTER THINGS

NEW BEGINNINGS, BETTER THINGS

"Let go … for better things to come into your life."

I learned an important secret from Buddhism.

If it comes, let it come.

If it stays, let it stay.

If it goes, let it go.

I'm flowing. I'm fascinated by challenging people and myself.

Since March 2022, I've been creating videos about challenging myself, sharing my philosophies about life, documenting my runs, filming my experiences, and talking openly on my platform.

A few of the challenges I did were:

- A seven-day dopamine detox, with no video games, no phone, no sex, no sugar, and no music. It was intense. I still ask myself how I managed seven days without any of these things! The video's called *I Did a Dopamine Detox for 7 Days Straight*.
- A three-day water fast. I had a knee injury because of running. I wanted to experiment to find out whether fasting could speed up the healing process. So, I tried fasting for three days, drinking water, and sharing the experience online. The video's called *I Healed My Knee with a Water Fast*.
- Twenty-four hours watching a timer. Yes, I sat in front of the TV for twenty-four hours straight, watching only the timer. I still laugh about this, but I did it. Twenty-four hours doing nothing besides looking at the timer. This video's called *I Watched the Timer for 24 Hours*.
- Jumping out of a plane. I was afraid of heights, so I decided to become a skydiver to overcome this fear. From the beginning of 2022 until the summer of that year, I spent most of my time in the drop zone, jumping out of a plane until I finally received my license and dissolved this fear. This video's called *How I Achieved a Dream I Always Thought Was Impossible*.
- One thousand pushups. I wasn't that fit back then, and a thousand pushups scared the s**t out of me. One day, I said to myself, "I'm going to do 1,000 pushups." My goal was to accomplish them, no matter how long it would take. It took me almost six hours, two naps, one meal in the middle, a lot of soreness, and endless roaring, but I did it. This one's called *I Did 1,000 Pushups in 24 Hours*.
- Turned $0 into $100. I spent a week selling one-on-one agendas that I created. I took all the money I gathered ($200), went to a car wash, met the guy who came to wash my car

and bought him clothes, games for his kid, and some groceries with the $200. This video's called *Why I Wanted to Turn $0 into $100*.

All these videos are on my YouTube channel, *@ramynaouss*. I know you'll watch and laugh. I wasn't sure what I was doing, and it's obvious in the videos, but I was trying. I was a kid exploring life. In those challenges, I learned so much about myself.

Remember, once you stretch your mind, it can never return to its original size.

Once, I did a seven-day dopamine detox. Spending twenty-four hours without my phone became a piece of cake. Try spending one day—only one—without your phone. The tranquility you feel will give you ultimate peace and calmness. Your life will never be the same, I promise you. Do a twenty-four-hour challenge without your phone, and send me a DM on Instagram. I'll be happy to hear about your experience.

Challenging myself unveiled a part of me that had been long buried or maybe wasn't there. I'm not sure. Once I began discovering myself, when I passed through the door and looked back, there was no door attendant. There was no going back to who I was. I kept exploring, trying, and experimenting.

I was scared, always doubting myself, and barely surviving financially. But I kept going like a kid who wasn't taking life seriously. In the end, I wasn't going to end up alive, right? What was the harm?

I ran my first kilometer barefoot in April 2022, and it was nice. I felt good. The next day, I went for a two-kilometer barefoot run. I enjoyed it.

I knew nothing about being barefoot or its advantages and disadvantages, but I wanted to experiment. I figured that in the worst-case scenario, my feet would hurt, and I'd go back to wearing my shoes.

In a century where you need socks, shoes, a watch, AirPods, a phone, a strap, shorts, t-shirts, and keys, I was running with just shorts. That was it.

It made an immense difference. Being barefoot is as human as one can be when running. It gave me a long-perished, magical feeling. I felt light. Words can't describe the actual feeling of being barefoot. It feels *free*.

I didn't attempt a twenty-kilometer run barefoot the very first time. I started off easy and improved slowly. The point is to take risks but be cautious while doing so. That's another secret about life: do crazy stuff, but cautiously.

I posted the story on my social media after my third barefoot run, and guess what people's replies were?

"Are you okay running barefoot?"

"Why barefoot, bro? What's wrong with you?"

"Bro, there are shoes for running."

"I'll buy you running shoes if you don't have them!"

All of these comments made no sense to me for a couple of reasons:

1. I don't believe in judging anyone or anything, because who am I to judge?
2. When you allow yourself to judge others, your opinion doesn't count if you've never been through the other's experience. Judging is egotism in action, and understanding is love in action.

If you're reading this, learn this lesson that took me twenty-eight years to discover: *People stuck in their minds are always judging others because they're scared to get out of their own minds.*

I believe in you, my friend, because you're reading this book and trying to improve somehow. We never judge. We always try to understand and learn.

By the beginning of May 2022, rising at 5:30 a.m. felt natural. I was finally a person who woke up at 5:30 a.m. It was no longer something I pushed myself to do; it happened naturally. Since January 20th, I'd been reading, learning, writing, meditating, running, growing, challenging myself, trying new experiences, trying new sports and activities, investing in myself, and building myself constantly. Brick by brick.

I tried researching barefoot running, but there wasn't much published science or knowledge about it. I was walking into a previously undiscovered world.

By that point, I was taking running seriously. I was improving and sharpening my skills. It was like most things in life—the better you become at something, the more passion you'll have for it.

If I'm happy, I run.

If I'm sad, I run.

If I'm stressed, I run.

If I feel bad, I run.

If I feel good, I run.

If I have too much on my mind, I run.

Running was a big part of my day. I posted a video about why I run on my YouTube channel, but my knowledge was minimal. This book is more interesting.

Looking back, I can see how the events of April 2022 shaped my life. I'd zoned in, fully focused with minimal distractions. I was running every day and reading one book a week. My meditation deepened, and I tasked myself with completing a big challenge each week. It was pretty intense. Effort is the only currency that matters in life.

I got lost within myself, not seeing my friends. I'd locked myself away in my Dubai apartment. My only concerns were my growth, self-development, and running. I've been working on self-improvement for two years. Eventually, my video content grew better, my ideas deeper, and my knowledge broader. My motto, *Let's Live*, was growing along with me.

Every day at sunrise, around 5:30 a.m., I ran barefoot on the streets. Every day, I posted my story and repeated my mantra. Chanting the same mantra daily helped me plant a positive seed in my brain. First thing in the morning, I focused on having a good day, regardless of challenges, problems, loneliness, financial shortages, and my solo efforts.

I was pushing forward and maintaining a positive attitude. Whenever I felt low—which is normal, I might add—I'd stop everything and sleep, whether early morning, noon, or afternoon. I'd wake up feeling better and try to push on once more.

> **A note for you:** *While in this phase, I had so much doubt, confusion, and fear about whether I was doing the right thing. Remember that the mind will always create these emotions when being pushed out of its comfort zone. Remember that it's almost impossible for your life not to improve when you spend time working on yourself.*

When you run five times a week, your heart, organs, and blood circulation improve. This affects your sleep, energy levels, and mental focus. Your stress levels decrease, and you become more resilient and a better human. This is a scientific fact.

My performances as a magician continued, but I wasn't improving my magic anymore. I was focusing on myself, my mind, my body, my ideas, and my approach to life.

I'd never felt so good in my life. Ever. I was mentally sharp and focused and had high energy levels throughout the day. I felt different. I'd become aware of and in tune with myself.

Those three years that I shared with you, I call *cave years*. I had a vision to become better, do better, and feel better. It started with no presumptions, only figuring out the next step and nothing further. That was until the journey shook the foundation of everything I knew about life—one day that redefined my life, beliefs, and whole being.

ONE MOMENT CAN CHANGE YOUR LIFE

"It only takes one moment to change your life forever."

As I continued with the challenges every week, an idea popped into my head. I decided to try a long barefoot run in Lebanon in the summer, figuring it would be a good challenge.

Well, that was the original idea. I didn't know what the distance would be or where I should do it. I only knew that I wanted to try barefoot long-distance running and support Lebanon somehow during its crisis.

How? When? Why? I had no idea yet. I was scared but excited and perhaps a little confused. There were so many mixed feelings all at once!

I took my phone to text my best friend, Zaher, whom I'm beyond grateful to have in my life.

I said, "Yo, bro, I have an idea."

He replied, "*Khair* bro. What's the idea?" ("Khair bro" is a Lebanese slang term used to express surprise while saying, "What's up?")

I said, "I'm thinking of running a long-distance barefoot in Lebanon this summer, trying to find an initiative and support my country, Lebanon."

What came next is the reason I love Zaher. He's always open-minded, never rejecting ideas.

Zaher asked me, "Did you try running long distances barefoot before?"

"No," I replied.

"Do you know who you want to support?"

"Not yet," I said.

Zaher responded, "Great! Let's figure it out. You prepare physically, and I'll check who we need to support. Let's do it, bro!"

I was ready. "F**k yeah, baby! Let's do it, bro."

There were three primary purposes behind the big idea:

1. It was a huge challenge and something I could add to my already accomplished list. I'd never run long distances

barefoot (actually, I'd never run long distances before). It was intriguing, and I was all in.

2. Whenever I'd go to Lebanon in the summer, I'd end up in a vacation mindset, which resulted in me getting drunk and high, wasting my time partying nonstop, sleeping late, spending the summer on the beach sipping wine, and so on. I'd been doing this for the past thirty years of my life. I wanted to try changing my approach, staying focused, and staying in my zone.

This challenge would motivate me to stay in the zone.

3. After COVID-19 and the subsequent economic crash in Lebanon, I had no way of helping my country. I was stuck in Dubai, broke and feeling useless. Why not try an act of kindness?

We took a week to think it through. A marathon is a decent distance barefoot. I calculated the distance from Beirut-Dbayeh (the starting point) to Batroun (the endpoint) as 42.5 kilometers. I also contacted my physiotherapist friend and requested a training program for my preparation.

I'd figured out around seventy percent of how, where, what, and the cause. One call with Zaher, and he was sold on the idea.

On June 20, 2022, I turned on the camera—still in Dubai—and recorded a video about my plans and the challenge and shared it on my YouTube channel. I was scared as f**k, but it was now a commitment. On July 24, 2022, I was going to run a marathon barefoot.

I spoke about the three reasons, unfiltered and imperfectly. The video didn't get much attention on YouTube, but it was a promise to myself, and I couldn't lie to myself.

I'll take this moment to thank my parents, who taught me life's most valuable lesson. They always used to emphasize how important it is to be honest in this world. Mom always used to tell me, "When a word comes out of your mouth, it's not just noise. It's a promise." Man! What a beautiful sentence and a delightful lesson! I'm grateful to have my parents and their outlook on life. Simply put, I love them.

Once I posted the video, I was in full-on training mode with one hundred percent focus. My good friend Elie Abou Moussa, a rehabilitation therapist and someone well-educated in sports, fed me all the knowledge required for the run, updated my training program, and followed up with me.

At the beginning of June 2022, my training became very serious, so if I had to complete two hours of cycling, I did it before the day ended. No excuses.

I had to run ten kilometers and then do strength and conditioning training. Whatever the program was, I refused to go to bed until it was done. I made the effort because I didn't want to pay the bill of regret.

A motto I live by that gives me peace in my life is, "Anything I decide to do, I do it wholeheartedly and give my best because if I fail and don't succeed, I don't want regret to fill my mind." When I do my best, and it doesn't happen, life shows me that's not the way. So I can change my direction without even the smallest amount of doubt.

This is another secret in this book—the secret that brought peace in my life in every decision I made. We'll talk about it later.

Discipline is a muscle; the more you use it, the more it grows. In his book *Can't Hurt Me*, David Goggins calls it "callus the mind".

When the power of will becomes strong, and your decision is followed by discipline, you become superhuman. You don't allow the mind to play games on you or stall you. The decision means there's no other option. Discipline means making sure it's done. This is power right here, bro.

I am not the mind. I am not the body. I am beyond physicality and logic. The true self (the soul) has no limitations on what's possible or real.

The soul decided to manifest in this world before the body and mind ever existed. Once you tap into your true self, the ego "I" becomes non-existent, and the mind and body follow the true self. Tapping into our true selves takes a lot of self-reflection, stillness, honesty, and effort.

In other words, it's through reading, writing, meditating, and running.

Remember, when I decided to run, I'd worked on my self-development from January 2020 until June 2022 and connected within—even when I was distracted and losing focus. No matter what, I kept trying.

What I just shared with you is something I didn't realize at the time. It was only recently that I was reflecting, assessing my life, and feeding myself with knowledge. Now I can share it with you because the picture is clear to me. I guess even though I was feeling them before, they were covered with layers of doubt, confusion, and fear.

The video I posted on YouTube received around five hundred views. The audience likely disregarded the video. They probably thought it was another bulls**t talk on social media or just another person in front of a camera. They were right, to be honest. A lot of people talk, but only a few walk their talk. For me, my purpose is a promise to myself.

Through my intensive training—long hours of cycling, running (long for me back then, between seven and twelve kilometers), strength training, and long stretching sessions—I was preparing myself for what was to come. I was loading twenty-four to thirty kilometers weekly and four to six hours of bicycling. Initially, it was challenging, and it started shaping me into what I am today. All my training and running were completed alone. Guess who I was talking to all the time …

I was talking to myself, observing my thoughts, and meeting my true self.

My mind tried to convince me to skip sessions or stop, but my true self kept on pushing until it was done. Every day.

While running long distances (whatever that is, based on your level), tuning in is a must. I noticed the three dimensions I was living in:

1. First, the body. While running, I was always scanning my body—the calves, the ankles, the knees, and the back—to check in and monitor for any injuries, whether minor or major, and I monitored my heart to see if it was beating at a normal or high rate.
   I'd also check my feet to see if they felt okay and check the surface I was running on to see if it was rough or whether I could maintain my stride on that surface.
   Everything that's happening within is related to the present. As I take the next stride and breathe the next breath, I'm in a moment of complete mindfulness, and my brain is sent into a meditative state. Its frequency changes: I call it an elevated state. Fully alert, the brain switches from a monkey mind to a monk mind. I was feeling a lot and learning a lot. With hindsight, I can now explain that as being the only difference.
2. Second, the mind. Meeting the devil inside my head, who was telling me I should stop or that I was tired and convincing me to bail, was a constant battle every time between my true self and the devil.

   I pushed daily to reach the target, winning most rounds. One day, the devil won in my preparation. It slipped, and he was actually able to convince me to bail on one of my workouts.

3. Finally, the soul. This is the real you that we'll speak about shortly.

During my training sessions, I learned to distinguish when the body was actually tired and not the mind convincing me that it was tired. This was critical because when my body is truly tired, and I push, I'll hurt myself and become the cause of all my injuries.

However, when the mind is playing games, trying to convince me that the body is tired and I push, there's no risk of injury. On the contrary, I could achieve what I was aiming for and—trust me—the body is so powerful, way beyond the mind's thinking.

At the beginning of July 2022, I traveled to Lebanon, continued my training, and stayed focused. Avoiding distraction in Lebanon was my main purpose from day one. The discipline in Lebanon remained the same, waking up at 5:30 a.m., sleeping early, training, and tunnel vision.

The beautiful part was that I was preparing for the challenge in my home country and next to my family.

My parents were surprised by my behavior. I'd changed from someone who was up all night and asleep all day to someone who was up by 5:30 a.m. and sleeping early. That was mind-boggling for them, honestly.

It's crazy how you can change and change your life!

The word got out two to three weeks before the marathon, and people around me knew I was preparing to run a marathon barefoot. I was always running barefoot and training. I wanted the soles of my feet to get stronger every minute of the day.

I heard a lot of this:

"This stupid man will hurt and embarrass himself."

I never cared and never will. Tunnel vision, baby.

In my preparations, my left knee sustained a minor injury. It was my weak point and another challenge to deal with. After every barefoot run, the soles of the feet need to recover.

A five-kilometer run required six hours for my feet to recover. For a seven-kilometer and ten-kilometer run, I needed around nine to ten hours to walk comfortably again. I learned all this along the way.

My life shifted because of these decisions and my intense training. Mornings became my best friend. I was eager for every sunrise, and peace took over all my life.

Remember! All you need is one good decision.

I personally don't take people's opinions to heart when I'm making a decision. Not because I'm smarter or arrogant but because everyone shares their opinion based on their values and personal experiences. I have a small circle of people whose opinions really matter.

People will share their opinions anyway, and these are some opinions they shared:

"When I ran a marathon, I prepared for six months; two months isn't enough."

"Running barefoot, you'll hurt yourself."

"Wear socks. Don't run completely barefoot. It's better for your feet."

"I don't think you'll finish the forty-two-kilometer run."

"Why run barefoot, bro? Why the struggle?"

Honestly, I don't see the opinions as negative. They're their beliefs, their limitations, and their perspectives. It has nothing to do with me.

I wanted to do it, which meant I'd experience it myself. I was ready for whatever came my way. I began building this mentality when I was diagnosed with cancer. I was the one struggling, I was alone, I was the one hurt, I was the one crying, and I was the one who dealt with it. People only felt sorry for me, and I despised anyone feeling sorry for me. I never felt sorry for myself, which was the same as in this situation.

To decide the starting and end points, I met a friend dear to me—a cancer survivor who founded an NGO called Crush Kancer with a Smile. We decided to collect the funds for his organization to support cancer patients who can't afford their treatment.

One week before July 24, 2022, I posted the official marathon video.

The video went viral, and my social media accounts were massively expanding. The accounts were on fire.

The video was beautiful, to be honest. It resonated with everyone; it delivered a message from my heart. All I'd done was tap in and try to improve myself, making my world slightly better, and the whole world supported me. Plus, cancer is a disease that takes away our beloved ones. People either face cancer or have someone close to them who was diagnosed. We all hate cancer. It's such a disingenuous disease.

I personally believe that the run gave everyone hope, starting with me.

This is another secret I want you to take from the book. Listen closely, as this is something I learned late: Anything that you do, do it with pure intentions, and make sure it originates from the heart. It touches people because we're all connected on a deeper level—it's our minds that disconnect us.

I received massive support from people all around the world. I was meeting people all over Lebanon, and people were sending videos running barefoot to support the run.

With all the exposure, my phone didn't stop ringing. I was contacted by news organizations, journalists, and so on, but I wasn't overwhelmed. I stayed calm and focused and mentally prepared myself for the run.

After all those cave days, inner battles, trying and failing, and trying again, I could finally see the light for the first time. It felt right.

DEVIL'S DAY

"For every new level, there is a new devil."

It was Saturday, July 23, 2022. One day before the run. It was the devil's day. The devil took control of my mind.

"You're going to hurt yourself."

"You're not ready for forty-two kilometers."

"You won't finish it."

"You'll embarrass yourself with failure."

Honestly, the devil knows when you're at your weakest and chooses that moment to make a move. When I encountered the devil, I was on my couch alone, feeling paralyzed, doubting myself, and wondering if the preparations had been enough. A wave of fear swept across my heart, and I questioned if I'd made the right decision.

I kept asking myself, *Did I make a wrong decision? Am I being reckless by doing this challenge?*

I didn't think it would become that big and the whole world would be watching. I'd been challenging myself and creating videos, yet I barely had a hundred views. Thoughts of *maybe I'm not ready*, *maybe I'll fail*, and *maybe it's too big a step* kept roaming in my mind. I was convinced I'd fail in front of everyone.

I was sitting on my couch. Three hours passed until the door opened, and Zaher came in.

"Ready, bro?" he asked, full of excitement with a big smile.

With a simple word and his great energy, all the nonsense in my head perished.

I stood up, and I said, "I'm f**king ready. Woohoo!"

We screamed for five minutes until we calmed back down again.

That night, I had dinner with friends and family and went to bed around 10:00 p.m. I was ready for the biggest challenge of my life.

PART 3

PATH TO SERENDIPITY

LIFE HAPPENS OUTSIDE OUR MINDS

"We're all going to die, so we might as well live. Let's Live."

On Sunday, July 24, 2022, I woke up at 3:30 a.m. My house was full of friends, and my family was next door. The energy and mood in the room were different.

I hopped in the car. After a seven-minute drive, we reached the starting point. More people were waiting for us at the assembly point.

I had tears in my eyes and was the only one truly able to understand why I was so emotional at that moment. Three years. Three years of putting in the effort, doubting myself, and being confused and scared until this day. Finally, I was able to see the fruits of my labor. This was the first time ever that I was actually high on life.

I warmed up for fifteen minutes, and at 4:46 a.m., I was in my starting position with forty-two kilometers ahead. It was time to focus. The past three years flashed before my eyes.

I looked at a camera in front of me and said, "I'm going to run a marathon barefoot, and all these amazing people are going to run with me."

I began the journey with Dad running to my left, three friends on my right, Mom driving behind me as a safety measure, my sister and other friends in the car in front, and Zaher and his brother on my left in a different vehicle.

I was running at a pace of 7.5–8 minutes per kilometer. The vibe was beautiful, and we were all smiling and enjoying the journey.

I looked at Zaher without speaking. We smiled at each other and nodded, as if we were silently acknowledging how this random idea from three months ago was actually happening right now with beautiful people surrounding us and amazing people from Lebanon and all over the world supporting us live on social media. All while we were supporting cancer patients.

I don't think I've ever been as close to being part of such a blissful act.

> *"We only live once, but if we do it right, once is enough."*

I was running slow and easy, feeling great as I covered the first ten kilometers and repeated my daily mantra: "Rise and shine, baby. It's a good day to have a great day. Woohoo!"

Before 2022, I laughed at people who said this person exudes "good energy" or "bad vibes". I was living in one dimension. How blind I was! Life stretches once you indulge in life, expand your knowledge and experience, and have an open mind. The day I admitted I had so much to learn about life, I became a student, learning every day. Life became bliss. As Socrates said, "The only thing I know is that I know nothing."

Back to my story. The energy of the day was so powerful. It was truly magical. Twenty kilometers in, I was feeling good, fueling my body with dates, bananas, and Gatorade (back then, I thought Gatorade was a good choice). My friends switched roles by my side, holding my water, passing me food, and driving by my side to protect me from the cars on the highway. Yes, I was running on the highway. An adult kid who was running surrounded by amazing people supporting him to achieve his goal. Our goal.

I'll take this moment to acknowledge how grateful and blessed I am to have my family and friends in my life and the unconditional love we share. My parents always advised me to do good and be good to people, and I did. I never had intentions to hurt anyone, even though I'm fully aware that I did hurt some people in the past unconsciously. However, since I started growing and developing myself and my life in 2020, I've made sure I'm good to everyone.

With all those people next to me on that day, I was speechless. Sometimes, I still wonder how it all happened. I guess it's life giving back to us.

Blessed.

The twenty-fifth kilometer. I remember that moment very well. I looked at my friend on my left, carrying my water and electrolytes.

I said, "I can go full sprint to Batroun (the endpoint) now."

He yelled back, "*Eh wleeee*!" which is typical Lebanese slang used to show support.

But little did I know what was coming next. After twenty-five kilometers, around 8:00 a.m., the sun was up, and my body entered a dark zone. A dark zone means a level never attained before.

At the twenty-eight-kilometer mark, my knees started getting tired, my ankles turned a bit sore, the asphalt beneath me had started getting hot, and my body was becoming drained.

Once you've been running for four hours, the body is already heating up and trying to cool itself. When you add in the heat from the sun, the heart needs to beat faster to control the body's temperature, which means more energy is needed. Without it, your body actually loses functionality, similar to the way your phone overheats.

At thirty kilometers in, I zoned in. My AirPods had been playing the same one-hour set on repeat (Rüfüs Du Sol). I wasn't hearing anything on the outside—I was focusing on every stride, thinking about the next step, and breathing fully in and fully out.

The devil started whispering, "You're tired." Man! The devil always appears at your low points.

I was in my zone, but the voice was becoming louder in my head.

"You will not finish!" the devil said.

Do you remember watching cartoons when the characters would have a devil sitting on their shoulder? I swear it was the same. It was as if the devil was literally on my shoulder with his voice loud and clear in my ear.

"You can stop now, and all the pain will go away," the devil said.

I silenced the devil with a quotation I kept repeating from the book *Lone Survivor* by Marcus Luttrell: "The body can take damn near anything. It's the mind that needs training."

Now we push. Tunnel vision, I thought to myself.

My mom was driving behind me, witnessing the whole journey, and I was thinking, *This woman gave me life, taught me life, and showed me life. I want her to be proud of this run, to be proud of her son, and to at least feel peace within that all her effort didn't go to waste.* Her effort matters. It made me the person I am today—the man running this run, the man who wouldn't stop until the fight is won, the man battling all odds, and the man who encounters cancer and understands the struggle of people diagnosed, waiting for their treatment and the challenges to be faced in the future.

"How you do one thing is how you do everything."

The run wasn't just about me. If I failed, all my friends, family, and everyone who supported me would fail. If I finished the run, we'd all win, and I'd win Mom's trust in my ideas and visions. Her support would be a blessing.

All the religious books talk about worshipping parents. Do good and worship your parents for a blissful life. Keep those words in the front of your mind.

Now, back to running. At thirty-three kilometers, I'd been fully focused for three kilometers. I'd almost reached thirty-four kilometers. My breathing became hard, my vision was blurred, and the pain was intense. I was overheating. Every nerve of my body told me to stop. The soles of my feet were damaged, and my muscles were tired, but I kept pushing. After pushing through the pain and soreness, I reached a breakthrough. I'd crossed my performance barrier big time (fifteen kilometers was my best before that day). It had been eight kilometers, and my muscles, thoughts, and gut were telling me to stop, but I kept going.

Then—and I'm not sure when exactly this happened—I felt different at some point during running. I was in a state I'd never felt before in my life. All the pain, soreness, and tiredness were gone. It was a state where time stopped. Nothing beyond that moment existed, and it was as if I was watching myself running, and it wasn't me who was running. I was fully aware. I'd reached a high state of consciousness, peace, and joy.

Look, I'm very curious, wanting to experience all parts of life and understand as much as I can grasp. That's why I was a magician before. I thought maybe I could do real magic if I became a good magician. That was until I encountered and felt real magic that day of the marathon—the magic of life. I let go of the tricks. I fell in love with the real magic of life.

During my thirty years, I'd tried everything, good and bad—trips and adventures, drugs, alcohol, and casual sex. All of it. But what I felt was completely different. Nothing in the world had made me feel what I felt during this run.

While I was in this state, I didn't know which kilometer I was on or where exactly I was. I was running. No, actually, I was *being*. That's it.

I was almost at the entrance of Batroun, around one and a half kilometers away from the finish line, when I snapped back to reality. There was a lot of honking and screaming, and people from everywhere were joining in for the last kilometer. My face showed all the signs of hurt and pain, but there were only a few strides left until I reached the tent prepared by Batroun municipality, which was the finish line.

Waves of emotions took over my whole body. Tears rolled down my face as I hugged my friends—my support system—one by one. Then, I saw Mom arrive alongside Dad and my sister. I hugged them and we were all crying. I was crying nonstop, and I didn't know why I couldn't hold myself together. (Later in this book, I'll explain why I was crying.)

I remember very well what was going through my mind at that moment. For the two weeks before the run, Mom was worried and had doubts about the run. She knew about my knee injury, and she was afraid that I might cut my feet on a piece of glass. To be honest, she was allowed to be worried. She's my mom.

She tried convincing me to take breaks, get my feet checked at each checkpoint, and get some rest in our car in case I was tired. Maybe she wanted to drive me to the next shaded spot. She was trying to make it all slightly easier on me. I completely understood where she was coming from. We've been programmed to avoid pain, but I made it clear.

"I'm doing it all the way, Mom. It's either all the way or nothing," I told her.

So, when I was hugging her at the finish line, I looked at her—no words—and we communicated through telepathy. *Mom, I'm sorry I wasn't the best son before today, but I promise things have changed. I've changed, and you can lean on me now with no doubt and no more nonsense. I'll take care of you and the whole family.*

If you watch the video on YouTube, you can actually see my face and the way I look at her after hugging her, as if I'm speaking, but there are no words. The video's called *I Ran a Marathon Barefoot*, and it's on my YouTube channel: @ramynaouss.

After all the hype, rest, and emotions, I thanked Batroun municipality for their support. We had some juice, took pictures, recorded a TV interview, thanked everyone, and went back home.

It was pure serendipity and a moment that will forever remain in the depths of my soul.

It was true that the run was over, but it was just the beginning. The feeling I described when I passed the thirty-kilometer mark—the high state of consciousness—took me eight months after the run to understand.

I'd gone through eight months of reflection, curiosity, constant learning, researching, and experimenting. I wanted to understand how it was even possible to feel what I felt, especially sober and without any substances. I remember very well that, at a certain point, it was an out-of-body experience.

No matter who asked me how the run was, my response was the same: "The most painful and blissful experience."

I've felt happiness, enjoyment, sadness, fear, and pleasure all my life. I thought I'd felt love, but actually, it was attachment. Yet I'd never felt joy, contentment, peace, and bliss. I was chasing women to feel validation and acceptance. I was buying new shoes and clothes to feel cool. I created a name, Raymi, to escape the uncomfortable feeling of my full name, Ramy Naouss, because I was bullied over my last name, Naouss, which means *sleepy*. I was double the size in terms of how I look today: big muscles to feel that I belonged with the cool crowd. I'd smoke a joint (actually, multiple joints) to feel high. That was the only way I thought I could get high. I was drinking to feel confident, to have the confidence to approach girls because if I was sober, I was insecure. I was always chasing a feeling on the outside.

But on this run, I had this feeling on the *inside*, triggered by immense physical challenge, struggle, and pain.

Wait, what? How was this even possible?

How on earth—when my mind is telling me to stop and when I'm enduring that much pain—could I feel my best? I couldn't fathom the fact that by pushing myself beyond my mind, I felt what I felt. The mind was what I knew, but there was a feeling beyond. Was there a different life outside my mind, and could I always feel like that?

ART OF CURIOSITY

"I have no special talents.
I'm only passionately very curious."

— Einstein

Twenty-four hours of fever, swollen feet, and sore muscles. I guess it's normal after running forty-two kilometers barefoot for the first time. Ten days later, I picked up the habit of running again. Slowly but surely. I knew that running was good for my health and everything else.

But no one told me about a high-conscious state. What does it mean? A high-conscious state? I thought only monks could reach a high-conscious state—or priests, or someone who could meditate for long hours. (I didn't reach a high-conscious state during my meditation, but it was making me feel good.)

I began a journey to understand this state, what it was, and how to reach it!

I went back in my mind to understand what made me reach it in the first place, how it affected my life, and how I could make it happen again!

> *"Once you see it, you can never unsee it."*

It was impossible to let go of what I felt or ignore the fact there was something there that I didn't understand. Do you think I could just go back to living my life before? Impossible, because I'm a curious man.

At the end of July, after the marathon, all the noise of "barefoot", "why barefoot", and all the judgments calmed down. People appreciated my efforts, especially when I announced that I accumulated $5,112 from the run and helped six cancer patients with the support of the NGO Crush Kancer with a Smile. I'd also been receiving DMs calling me a hero. It touched me, man! I swear my plan was just to challenge myself to become better, and if I could help someone, that would be even better.

I've shared some of the challenges I've gone through. I'd helped people before, but this one was different. I guess it was life testing me to determine whether I really wanted to improve or was just doing it to get views. After I'd persevered for three years, life gave me what I deserved—the support I needed to keep elevating.

I'm beyond grateful.

In August, I was back into my morning routine, running barefoot again, reading, meditating, and wondering what was next for me. That wasn't an easy question, mostly because the previous challenge was a big one. Maybe I was this one-hit wonder, and I'd disappear. Every interview, I was pressured with the question, "What's next, Ramy?"

I had no idea. I was just a simple man trying to become better. I did a video on my YouTube discussing this phase. It's called *Overthinking is Ruining My Life, Here is How I Escaped*.

If you watch the video, you can tell I was a bit lost, speaking to the camera about my doubts and overthinking. I suggest you watch the beginning and the end of the video. You'll understand the point I'm trying to make and maybe it will give you some insights if you're overthinking.

One thing I learned, and it's my strength when I get lost or confused, is that I could disconnect from the outside world and spend time with my family and friends, tap into my morning routine, and all the fog would disappear.

At the end of November 2022, I was back in Dubai. I usually go back there earlier, but I'd stayed in Lebanon for six months that summer because Mom needed me. It was a hard time for all of us, and I wanted to be around them as much as possible. (I'll share more info about this matter later in the book.)

As soon as I was in Dubai, I was back to my morning routine—early rising, running, reading, writing, meditating, and so on.

I know I'm emphasizing my morning routine, but I want you to know that's how I changed my life. Jim Rohn said in his speeches, "Work on yourself more than you work on your job." I was working on myself more than my magic or anything else.

My life consisted of learning, acquiring knowledge, refining my skills, writing my thoughts, and creating content on social media. I mention creating content here because the discipline and consistency of creating content every day pushed me to keep growing. I didn't want to share lame stuff. I wanted to deliver value. How would I deliver value? By becoming more valuable.

During this phase of my life, I understand my motto, *Let's Live*, in depth. I'd always thought it was clear in my head, but actually, it wasn't. After the summer, something felt different, and maybe that was what it meant. I was still on a path of discovery.

One thing's for sure: I was aware that the more I challenged myself, the more I felt alive, so Let's Live was taking a new, clear direction. It's not just two words, but a vivid path of how someone can feel alive. The image wasn't completely clear in my head, though it was somewhere to dig deep.

On the other hand, I was on a mission to understand the state I reached in my run, with many questions not answered yet.

This motivated me daily, so I ran five times a week, read books, searched on the internet, understood what consciousness was, looked into the meaning of elevated states, reflected, analyzed every run, and basically lived with intention.

Once you run forty-two kilometers barefoot, you unlock the mind. Five kilometers became a warm-up. My runs started taking a new shape: five kilometers turned into seven kilometers, then seven kilometers turned into ten kilometers, and ten turned into fifteen kilometers.

Eventually, running stopped being a workout for me. It became a lifestyle. I didn't have to be disciplined anymore; it was as if my body pushed me to run, especially since there was something in those runs—a feeling yet to be unlocked.

I swear the day I ran a marathon barefoot was the day that made me believe that I'd touched life, or maybe life had touched me. I was in a situation that allowed it to happen because of running; I thought better, I moved better, I felt better, and I did better. I'm a better human overall, and running made me fall in love with this human dimension. Still, there's a lot left to discover.

PART 4

A NEW START AND MANY POSSIBILITIES

NEW YEAR, NEW ME

"If you change, life will change."

On December 31, 2022, I'd been invited to perform magic in the Buddha Bar for New Year's Eve. I was still doing some shows here and there. It was my hobby that generated cash as well.

I arrived at 8:30 p.m. to prepare myself. My show was at 10:15 p.m. on stage, and then I'd be roaming around the guests' tables until 11:45 p.m.

I'd like to take this moment to inform you that before 2022, I'd never ever *not* been drunk on New Year's Eve. Never. But on this night, I was drinking only water and following my feelings.

I finished my stage act, then accomplished my roaming performance. It was 11:50 p.m. I was with my good friend, a general manager. I waited until midnight. It was officially 2023. We hugged. I had so much love for her. We wished each other a happy new year, and I headed back home. By 12:30 a.m., I was in bed, ready to sleep, not quite believing that I was one hundred percent sober. At 7:00 a.m. on January 1, 2023, I was on the streets running, hitting my ten kilometers. This run was different because no one was on the streets. Even the birds took a day off from flying. It was the ultimate bliss. I'd never seen the streets of Dubai that silent. I was high on life and chasing what made me tick. So much power was packed into that day.

Since this run, I understood that 2023 wouldn't be like any other year. I could feel it, and I was ready for it.

I went home after the run to sit, read, and reflect on how I'd be approaching the year. At noon, I reached for my phone to check Instagram. I came across an advertisement for a ten-kilometer race in Dubai Creek on January 22, 2023. I registered immediately.

That month, my content took a new form. I was expressing my thoughts unfiltered and talking about how to live a good life in a very *edutaining* way. One of the videos went viral, reaching seven million views. My platforms blew up. It was like everything was falling into place, brick by brick. Trust me, it's not about the views; it's about being aligned with the vision, the goal, the efforts, the health, the hustle, the surroundings, and the results. None of the above is a success on its own. Success is a compound effect. If you are rich in the bank but not close to your family, you're a failure. If you have the best car and house in the world but are in bad shape, you're a failure. If you have the best vision and work ethic but don't have love, you're a failure.

I was going viral with waves of DMs. People sharing stories with me about how my content was helping them improve, become better, and discover themselves touched me deeply. It was another push. I guess this time, life was confirming that I was doing the right thing.

On Sunday, January 22, at 5:45 a.m., I was at the starting point. It was my first time participating in an event like this. With good vibes and good people all around me, I was experiencing a new type of event in my life. All my previous runs were alone, but running alongside other people felt good.

At 6:00 a.m., the whistle went, and I started running. I wasn't racing or competing with anyone; I was competing against myself. I was excited, and my adrenaline was at its peak. I was trying to control the pace so I didn't run too fast. The first two kilometers should be nice and easy so your heart and veins warm up properly.

After the third kilometer, I let myself go. I freed my body to run of its own accord. I was flowing; my pace was five minutes per kilometer, which was a decent pace, but I didn't feel I was running. It felt more as if I was flying. At the sixth kilometer, I started crying while I was running. I wondered what was happening to me. With every run, there were chapters of crying, and I couldn't understand what was happening within. I was letting it be. Later, I understood that crying is a way of healing. So, with every run, I was healing. More on this later.

Running is bliss—how it affects the body and the brain. There's nothing close to running. It's not just a workout but a dimension to travel within, understand oneself, heal, and grow. Imagine what happens while running barefoot, when your sensory system is connected to the soles of the feet, directly in contact with Mother Earth.

We humans as a species interact with the earth through our feet. We don't take naps on grass, chill on a tree, or immerse ourselves in sand every day. (Maybe occasionally.)

Nowadays, many studies, notably Gary Brecka in his latest studies and podcast, show how grounding (walking barefoot on grass and sand) affects our physiology, makes our red blood cells active, discharges negative electrons, and boosts our immune system. I have to give you that information. Trust me, it matters. It benefits you.

We are animals with consciousness, so it's a must to be connected to Earth. As part of nature, we can't keep avoiding it and wondering why we're not feeling good. Check how you feel sitting in your room the whole day and compare it to when you're on the beach, walking outdoors, or in a park. It does matter. So, stop ignoring reality. I'm not saying go completely barefoot and live an extreme life like mine. *No.* Instead, find a balance, and you'll improve your quality of life. First and foremost, you'll feel good and healthy. All the rest comes after.

I'm aware of my body. I know, and I feel how my mind and body discharge when I'm outdoors. That's another secret that improved my quality of life.

Spend more time outdoors. That's the secret.

Back to the run. My tears dried, and I was still running, breathing, and fully present. I felt this transcendence, much lighter, but I was touched by it again. I was in an elevated state, loving everything, feeling everything, and being one with everything.

I was touched by life.

I'll try to explain what it means to be touched by life. It's difficult to put into words because you have to feel it, but I'll try.

Remember when someone said something good to you, a time you did something that felt so right and made so much sense, a location you once went to, or a moment spent with someone you loved. You get goosebumps, your head tingles from the top down, all the neurons in your system are on fire, and you get this rush of emotions. That's what I call being high on life. It was as if a drop exploded in my head, and I could feel every bit of my body.

I finally finished the ten-kilometer run in fifty-one minutes, which was a new personal record.

On that day, everything that was happening in my life felt right. I cried because I was in awe of life. I was finally at peace within. Nothing had changed yet from the outside, but I felt joy within. I felt that everything was making sense—my change, the new me, my new lifestyle, and *Let's Live*.

I knew it was only the beginning, and now it was time to push. When three years of effort start to manifest, it's time to stay focused and not take a break.

My intuition was guiding me to my next big challenge, and guess what it was?

Let's jump to the next one!

PART 5

FIND STRENGTH IN PAIN

PAIN IS THE WAY

"Avoid pain, it will hunt you.
Go to pain, it will heal you."

I stood on a nail board, also known as a *sadhu* board, for the first time in mid-2021. My first attempt was hilarious; I could barely stand for fifteen seconds. Yet the feeling I had was unlike anything else. How could a couple of nails positioned in a particular way make me feel immense pain when nothing was actually hurting me? I was curious. I immediately told my yoga instructor to get me one. Two days later, the nail board was in my room.

I started experimenting with it, standing on it for twenty seconds the first day, pushing for thirty seconds the next, and so on. In a couple of months, I could stand on the board for a minute.

When I began barefoot running, I was eager to learn more about the feet, the health benefits, and how it affected my life. One thing I discovered when I stood on the nail boards for a minute before my run was that I was activating my feet, which was helping with my barefoot running. There's neither much information online about the correlation between the two, nor a lot of information about each by itself. So, I took the initiative to learn about the two, acquire enough knowledge, and create data in my journal.

During the summer of 2022, I stayed in Lebanon for six months. My auntie's (Mom's sister) cancer relapsed after being in a six-month remission, but this time it was terminal. The hardship of knowing that your beloved has only three months left to be alive is sorrowful. I'm very close to Mom, so I wanted to be by her side through this phase. Trust me, from the day of my auntie's terminal diagnosis until the day she passed away, I saw Mom struggle every single day. She was in tears, felt sad and depressed most of the time, and forgot about herself. I was always hungry to find a way to make this phase easier on her, but there was no way. There was only one way to deal with it, and that was to accept it and be by her side. That I did.

In December 2022, I was back in Dubai while my family was in Lebanon. My auntie was in Australia (where she lived with her children). During that time, I felt like my heart had been chopped into pieces and spread around the world. All the pain I'd been feeling since the summer was growing within.

People say that time heals all wounds. It's a lie. Time *buries* all wounds, but the cut is still there. Unless you dig deep, address the pain, deal with it, accept all the baggage that comes with it, and keep doing this for some time, you can't heal the wounds. Trust me, it's not only time that matters.

I've met people, my friends, and my best friends, and we worked together to heal their wounds. We tapped into wounds created so long ago that they even forgot they were there. However, they had never healed and had only been buried until we addressed the issue, solved it once and for all, accepted how the trauma shaped us, and dealt with it. Then, the wounds were healed.

Back to December. All the pain was building in me—the pain of the future death of my aunt and the pain of seeing my mom struggle. Running was really helping at that time, but something inside me felt icky.

The nail board was always in my room next to my bed. The day before Christmas Eve, feeling very low, I stood on the nail board for one hour. My knowledge is minimal, but remember, I wasn't well. I felt heavy, and something was telling me to stand on the nails. I screamed, roared, breathed, shouted, and pushed for the first ten minutes. Then I felt numb; I got comfortable in the uncomfortable. When you stand on the nail board, pain takes the shape of waves—peaks and lows—but every phase lasts just a couple of minutes.

After standing on the board for an hour, my inner pain had been unloaded. I felt lighter.

Another realization. *Healing pain means going through the pain!*

In January 2023, I was experimenting with the nail board in depth. I created a schedule of loading six hours per week divided across the week. I planned for one hour on the first day, thirty minutes on the next, rest on the third day, two hours on the fourth day, thirty minutes on the fifth day, two hours on the sixth day, and rest on Sundays.

Because my feet were always exposed to asphalt, sand, and grass, my improvement was exponential. In one session of my morning routine, I was standing in stillness with my eyes closed, and an idea popped into my head. *Stand long hours on the nail board.* I finished my session and reflected on the thought.

As I did before the marathon, I decided to speak to Zaher.

Zaher asked, "What's your best so far?"

"Two hours," I replied.

"What's your aim?" he asked.

"I don't know. Maybe twelve?"

Zaher asked, "Why twelve?"

"Twelve months represents a cycle of life. Every cycle contains the ups (enjoyment, happiness, comfort, and contentment) and the downs (pain, struggles, sorrow, and grief). If I stand for twelve hours, I believe I'll feel all those emotions."

"True," Zaher agreed.

"Plus, my auntie isn't well. Maybe I can set a world record in honor of her."

Zaher said, "I support the idea. I'm not going to ask if you can do it. Just inform me if there's anything I can do."

"I'd reach out to Guinness. There's a similar record of someone standing on a bed of nails. Maybe I can break this record or set a new one," I said.

"Let's do it. Tell me when you want to do it, so I can book a flight to Dubai," Zaher replied. He lives in Lebanon.

In retrospect, I thought I wanted to set the record for my auntie, but actually, it was for Mom. My auntie is a very tough woman. She accepted her death and planned parties every day until the end, when she'd have to go to the hospital. She gave tasks to each family member to do when she was gone. She was the one who planned her funeral, and she said "love life" every day. Her life is an inspiration to me. She touched me deeply. I love you, Auntie.

My mom was the one facing the burden, the grief, and the sorrow.

Like when I was diagnosed with cancer, my family took the shock and the pain. I recovered mentally in a short period, but it took Mom three months to accept the reality.

Life is not about you.

I thought standing on nails would give hope to the whole family during a tough period.

I began the journey to prepare for the twelve hours. I had no idea how I'd do it or what was required from me physically. I reached out to my auntie and shared the idea with her; she loved it. We made a video together. I announced the challenge while she was explaining her case.

By the end of January 2023, I was totally focused on my runs and the nail board. I had a feeling that everything was falling into place. My understanding of the nail board had grown. I made plenty of mistakes that I adjusted.

Some of them were:

1. I was standing on the nail board and watching TV. When facing pain, you must be in tune with yourself and calm, not watching TV and allowing distractions.
2. It's very important to empty your bladder before standing on the nail board and understand what's in the gut.
3. What to eat and how to fuel your body are very important.
4. If the brain is agitated, staying on the board for long gets very hard.

I learned all this by myself. Every time I finished a session on the nails, I wrote down what I learned, what mistakes I'd made, and how I could improve.

By the end of January, I'd decided on the challenge date. It would be March 5, 2023. My auntie was still feeling fine, and with another month, I was sure I'd figure out the rest so I could complete the challenge.

I applied to Guinness, but the application could take twelve weeks, and I didn't have the time. Auntie's situation was critical.

Luckily enough, the Guinness Board replied in three weeks. It was all God's plan.

They advised me on what was required, how to film, how to show evidence, and all the necessary details.

I proceeded with the plan.

This is how my life looked in January 2023:

- My diet included 1,800 Kcal per day of clean, organic food rich in fruits and vegetables.
- I ran every day.
- I did strength training in the gym for three days a week.
- I did six to eight hours per week on the nail board.
- I spent long hours meditating every day.
- I breathed and stretched daily.
- I was writing and reading to expand my knowledge.

The area surrounding my apartment was full of parks, green spaces, and a calm beach. I was living like a monk but in a huge city like Dubai.

In February, I pushed the bar to new limits. It was similar to January, except I had to slow down on running, as I wanted this month to be fully prepared for the nail board record.

Standing for long durations on a nail board is completely different from running. Running involves a high heart rate, high tempo, high action, and uplifting music, while standing on nails needs a low heart rate, calmness, and relaxation.

My days became peaceful and much calmer with longer meditations, breathing sessions, less food, and fasting for long periods. My pain threshold improved. I delved into pain—physical pain and emotional pain—and believe me, physical pain is the easiest one.

By February, my digestive system was super-clean. The energy I felt all day was unmeasurable. There was a clarity in my mind that I'd never felt before. The flow of my emotions and how I felt was unexplainable. I felt sad, but it didn't stick. Waves of emotions came and went, and I just observed them. I was elevated. I told myself, "I am not the emotions. I am not my thoughts. I am." That's it.

Endorphins are released to help you survive and relax when your body feels pain or stress. When you feel pain, nerves send pain signals to your brain. Your brain releases endorphins to block the nerve cells that receive the pain signals. Endorphins are neurotransmitters released by the pituitary gland and hypothalamus in the brain. As natural hormones, they can alleviate pain, lower stress, improve mood, and enhance your sense of wellbeing. The body releases endorphins when you engage in pleasurable activities, such as eating, exercise, and sex.

During that month, I discovered how I detached from my emotions and pain, which allowed me to take my nail board challenge to another dimension.

Once, in mid-January, I tried to stand for six hours while watching TV and being on my phone. At the five-hour mark, I was in immense pain, and I was very agitated. I went down after five hours and fifteen minutes. I failed.

At the beginning of February, with my knowledge, discoveries, and leveling up, I attempted to stand for six hours on the nail board, meditating, breathing, and being present and aware of the pain without reacting to it.

I accomplished six hours, but there was tremendous pain afterward. I experienced fifteen minutes of screaming and roaring to rid myself of the pain.

A fun fact: When I'm on the nail board, my nervous system is under a lot of pressure. When I get off the nail board after a long session, the nervous system fires up, similar to how it hurts when you sit in an uncomfortable position on your leg for ten minutes and then stand. It's like you're paralyzed, but a hundred times worse.

Once the extreme pain faded, I slept for three hours to recover. It was at this stage that I started to understand how food would affect my pain tolerance. I'd also learn how to fuel my body, how to control urges to use the bathroom, and how to maintain good energy levels throughout the full session.

The lessons I learned on the nail board are lessons that no school, university, or wisdom could have ever taught me.

Here's a major discovery I made during my long hours standing on the nails. There are two types of states we experience in our lives:

1. A low-level human state (I gave it this name) is when you're stuck on silly thoughts like *I'm hungry* or *I'm bored*, or even regretting the past, avoiding the self, and dwelling in lame conversations about gossip, negative talk, and arguments.
2. A high-level human state is when you think things like *I am grateful to be alive*, or *I am watching the tree and the birds, appreciating every moment I'm in*, or perhaps projecting the future in a positive introspect, expressing love and observing with no judgments.

These discoveries came after two months of assessing every session, spending some time in ultimate silence and listening to the thoughts of others on the phone, collecting data, and saving it.

I often called my mom while standing on the nail board during my long sessions. We had beautiful conversations, some of which made her smile. I gave her hope just by standing on nails, feeling her pain somehow.

Other times, I wanted to stop mid-session, but I reminded myself, "I'm experiencing this pain for a limited time. As soon as I get off, it will be gone," which kept me going. The thought that my auntie could never escape her pain was my motivation to keep pushing every day, because I could choose to step off the nails, and the pain would go away, but for her, there was no choice.

Another day aiming for a long session, but nothing went as planned. Though, in the end, everything happened as it should.

PART 6

WHAT YOU ARE SEEKING IS SEEKING YOU

ALL THE ANSWERS ARE WITHIN

"If you keep searching, you will find."

On February 19, 2023, I woke up at 6:00 a.m. I was on a twenty-four-hour fast; my stomach was empty. I prepared some fruits and fuel for a seven-hour session standing on nails. I went to the bathroom to empty the bladder and placed the nail board in front of my balcony, a space I created to see the trees, the streets, and the green space ahead.

At 6:45 a.m., I placed one foot on the board, followed by the next. I closed my eyes and started breathing (a three-second inhalation, then a six-second exhalation; it relaxes you instantly—try it!). After an hour, I was feeling good. I was high on my breath and endorphins, but my feet started shaking. I tried to fight it off, but the more I fought it, the weaker they became until I reached a point where I couldn't stand anymore. A war broke out in my head. *I have to step down. No. I have to complete seven hours.* It went on and on until my whole body started shaking.

I got off, lay down on my bed, still shaking, and I started crying. I cried a river. I closed my eyes, and I became lost within, seeing images of Mom, my sister, Dad, and my friends whom I love. The faces of the people that I truly admired flashed in my head. I saw my childhood and moments stuck within as if I was watching my life on a screen. At that moment, I was an observer of my life.

Seeing everything inside me and all the memories in my subconscious and unconscious mind—every time someone called me skinny, every time I felt like a failure, every time I felt weak, every time I felt guilty—was a rollercoaster ride, but I wasn't judging myself or trying to control anything. I was in my bed, crying and letting go.

I accepted and surrendered to whatever had happened in my past. If I'd been dying, I would've been okay with death.

I have no idea how long I was in this state. Once my tears dried, I opened my eyes and felt ecstatic (shedding emotional tears releases oxytocin and endorphins, elevating your state of mind and making you feel good). I stood up and looked in the mirror, loving the person I saw despite being skinny, despite the mistakes I made in the past, and despite who I was.

I was loving this awareness. I loved myself. I loved my family. I loved my friends. I loved everyone and everything. I loved this existence, and I loved life. I felt blessed to be alive.

I stared at myself for a while, then I felt the urge to run. I put on my shorts and went for a run without my shoes. No phone, no headphones, nothing. Just my shorts. I was on the street running, but this day, I wasn't running to a certain destination, and I wasn't running away from anything. I passed the park, I ran to the beach, and I ran back home. While I was running, I felt the vibrancy of life. I noticed how the sky was moving, almost melting in front of my eyes. I was feeling the earth, stamping my feet with every step. I loved the fact that I was barefoot. I'll always run barefoot because it allows me to feel the energy of everything around me. I was one with Earth, with nature, and with the sky. I became everything and nothing.

If you're wondering how all this happened, understand that life is a compound effect. Nothing happens in life for just one reason. Success, growth, failure, sickness, and bliss … It has taken years of effort and hard work, reading, meditating, running, and challenging myself constantly. I was always satisfied but never settled. I pushed myself outside my comfort zone daily, physically, mentally, and spiritually. My digestive system and body were very clean. I was at my healthiest and more in tune with myself than ever.

I expanded my knowledge of the physiology of the human mind and the brain. I studied a lot of monks and people who'd reached a high level of consciousness. I was and still am a seeker and a curious kid. The nail board was an instrument that helped me dig deeper. I genuinely believe that this day was the result of the four previous years and an answer to all the questions I had previously. It was the outcome of planting, nourishing, fixing the environment, letting go of my past, and striving to become more. It was a result of all my effort.

Through my runs, I wondered, *Where the f**k was I before?*

Unaware of myself, disconnected from the world. *Was I even a human before?*

On this day, I felt what it means to be a human—healthy, happy, strong, powerful, and loving. I was ready to receive, but I was beyond ready to give with zero numbness and one hundred percent awareness.

Before this, I was a lost man, stuck in my own mind. It was a mind of negative emotions like guilt, shame, and feeling sorry for myself. I was lazy, work-avoidant, and selfish.

Since 2020, I'd been trying to push beyond the mind with the small amount of knowledge that I had at the start. I was trying. I was putting in the effort.

People asked me, "Are you out of your mind, running barefoot?"

I never knew how to reply before this day. "Of course I was outside my mind. Living inside my mind was stealing the beauty of life."

I returned home after sunset in a state of ultimate blissfulness. I lay in bed again, closed my eyes, and drifted off to sleep.

You and I are the same. We have to stop searching for what differentiates us and start looking at our similarities. Trust me, we're all the same. Our minds and the ego mind separate us, but deep within, we are one. We're conscious animals, and it's your duty, as it is mine, to tap within, feel ourselves, feel each other, and feel the earth, life, universe, and God. We're one organism in different forms ... we're the same tree and a different branch.

You and I are Earth, and Earth is us. Seventy percent of our body is water. Seventy percent of the earth is water. When we have a fever, we sweat; when the earth is hot, it rains. Inside our stomach, there is a world beyond our understanding; the microbiota in our gut is an ecosystem similar to the one found in nature. The plants offer meals of sugars, vitamins, organic acids, and phytochemicals to the soil. In return, the soil bestows the plant with a nurturing microbial environment in the same way that food enters your gut. Look at your eyes and the form of the universe; they're alike.

It's beyond our understanding, bro.

I was mesmerized by these thoughts. Life itself is spectacular.

We are the only species who know we exist and can think and assess. Other living beings, such as dogs, birds, and plants, feel they're alive, but they don't *know* they're alive (that's what we know so far).

Why are we the only ones who are aware of life? I was still trying to figure it out.

PART 7

ACCEPTANCE IS THE KEY

ACCEPT WHAT LIFE HAS TO OFFER

"Accept what comes your way, learn to walk with it.
The more you avoid, the more you will be chased."

I woke up the next day as if I was reborn and got straight back to training on the nail board. I had one last challenge I needed to overcome before March 5, 2023. Every time I was on the nail board for several hours, I needed to go to the bathroom. I started studying how the digestive system functions to understand how I could overcome this challenge.

Basically, every time you go to the toilet, you're letting go of what you ate thirty-six hours prior. That was the information I needed. When you use the bathroom, your body is removing waste, so if you eat the high-quality food that your body needs, you don't need to go to the bathroom as often. It was a big realization for me.

I fasted for thirty-six hours before my long periods of standing. After my fast was complete, I'd go to the bathroom and then go to the nail board. Once I was on the nail board, I started fueling.

I posted the video on my Instagram. It's titled *I'm Going to Set a World Record Standing on Nails for More than 12 Hours on 5th of March. I'm Doing it for My Aunt.* The video shows a switch where my aunt explains her case in detail. The video ends with me saying, "Let's live, baby."

The power that a video has, at least for me, is great. It's a promise with a deadline. It's the secret to growth.

On February 21, 2023, two days after the day that I was reborn, I was aiming for eight hours on the nail board. I was well-prepared mentally and physically. I'd fasted, and I prepared my own meals. I spent nine hours breathing, meditating, and reading. I then called my mom and talked to her for forty-five minutes, observing the people on the streets. On that day, I watched people leave for their jobs and saw them return home while I was still standing. I learned how to observe others in the same way that I observe myself, with no judgment. I fueled every hour with my meals and snacks. At eight hours, I felt elevated, so I decided to go for one more hour. My mind, body, and soul were in harmony. I wasn't standing. I was actually flying.

After accomplishing nine hours, it was time to remove my feet from the board and endure the immense pain for the next twenty minutes. I took my first leg off and then the second (this actually takes ten minutes by itself). The nervous system is released shortly after the removal, and it's time for screaming and roaring. I actually posted a story on my Instagram, and people were messaging me asking why I was doing this to myself. It made sense to me, but that doesn't mean it had to make sense to anyone else, though you know the story behind it now. I was doing it for Mom, my auntie, my family, and for everyone struggling with pain. I feel you. It was beyond a record and beyond the video. It was personal. A fire ignited deep within.

A few more tests and I was all set. Here are the details of the plan:

1. The challenge was on Sunday, March 5. Thursday's lunch would be my last meal.
2. I'd dropped six kilograms for the challenge so I'd be lighter on the nail board.
3. I'd completely disconnect myself from the outside world, beginning on Friday. There'd be no phone, no YouTube, and no distractions. Only calmness, silence, and piano music.
4. I'd drink plenty of water to flush out all toxins from my system.
5. On Saturday at 9:00 p.m., I'd stop drinking water.
6. I'd prepare three meals of fruits (avocado and honey) and small amounts of liquids, so there'd be no need to use the bathroom while on the nail board.

I booked flights for the whole family to be by my side on the day of the challenge.

On Sunday February 26, I was all set.

On Tuesday morning, my auntie wasn't well and was taken to the hospital. No matter how much you prepare for death, it will always shake your foundation.

Mom sent me a text: "I think this is it."

I'm not someone who escapes reality by any means, and especially in this case, I can't tell Mom, "No, don't say that." We all know the truth. I sent her a heart with no words.

I woke up the next day (Wednesday, the fourth day before the official challenge day), and Mom had sent me a text: "She's gone." I called her straight away.

Goshhhh …

My heart split in half, hearing the grief in Mom's voice. I have only one wish now … My wish is that I'll eventually be the one to bury Mom and that she'll never be the one burying me; that's all I ask. The pain was agonizing and was nothing compared to any physical pain I ever felt.

I kept calm and strong while speaking to Mom. As soon as the phone call ended, I collapsed. No matter how long I'd been preparing for this moment, it was a reality check. The Angel of Death won't spare anyone. Some are earlier than others, but every time you meet death, it's another wake-up call.

"We all know that we're going to die, but no one believes it because the day you believe it, your life will never be the same."

I cried endlessly, and at the same time, I was confused about what to do with the challenge. Should I postpone? Should I cancel? Should I cancel my parents' flight? What should I do?

Here, I want to take a moment to thank my friends, whom I call family in Dubai, who stayed by my side during this critical time.

My brother-by-choice, Jhony, arrived a few moments after receiving the news. He advised, "Take this day to grieve. Don't make a decision today; accept what happened."

I nod, silent.

He adds, "That is what life has for you ... you don't postpone. You do it for your auntie, your mom, and the whole family."

I used to get stressed when things didn't go my way. But since my self-discovery journey, I've learned that the secret to a good life is to accept what flows into your life and move forward.

The next day, I went for a walk. I walked to the closest park without my phone. Before interacting with the world, I climbed my favorite tree and sat peacefully. I felt that the right thing to do was what Jhony advised.

Making decisions is one of the most challenging skills I've nurtured over the past years. I was always afraid that I was making the wrong decision. Here's the truth. There's no right or wrong decision! I make a decision based on a feeling that I get about the decision. Intuition. Believe me when I say we have a power beyond our minds, but we must be in tune with it.

I follow my intuition, make the decision, and handle the consequences. Escaping decisions is avoiding reality, avoiding life, and avoiding growth. I follow this system whenever making decisions. I assess them after a month, and it usually shows that it was a good decision.

Every big decision is scary, and it's going to feel extremely uncomfortable, but that's the only way.

I posted a video on my social media. In it, I'm in tears as I announce the death of my auntie and inform viewers that I'll stick to the date that had been set for the challenge. Unfortunately, I had to postpone my family's tickets. They had to stay in Lebanon for the funeral and to provide support to the bigger family.

On Thursday, I ate my lunch and entered my long fast. For the next seventy-two hours, I only had to drink water, sleep, disconnect, and be in isolation.

Fasting heals on a physical level (proved by science) and on an emotional level (no need for science to prove it to me). I've felt it. I've experienced it. You go into an altered conscious state and become so in tune with yourself. Think about it ... the body and the gut, after six hours, have nothing to digest, so they start cleansing the small intestine, the large intestine, the liver, and the pancreas. You're actually resetting the digestive system.

Your mind isn't thinking about food. It's a huge, empty mental space. Your senses are alert. You tune to the body, not the mind.

At this time, the mind will look for the easiest dopamine hit or the easiest distraction, but when you're out of food for more than sixteen hours, the body takes over.

I was lost within. I was in tune with myself, with no Instagram, no YouTube, and no people. I wasn't scared, and I had no doubts. I was silent, calm, and waiting for Sunday.

ALL SET AND DONE

*"I accomplish it in my mind,
then I make my body follow."*

It was Sunday, March 5, 2023. The day had finally arrived. I woke up at 5:00 a.m. My friends had slept over. I was calm with almost seventy-two hours of no food and zero distractions. I was in Zen mode.

We reached the location by 5:45 a.m. and started testing the camera (the challenge needed to be recorded for twelve hours nonstop to provide evidence to Guinness).

We all gathered. There was me, Zaher, Isabella, Jhony, Dima, Ashraf, and the Kamal Eldine family, who hosted the location.

I said, "I already feel it. It's going to be a good day to have a great day."

I took my position, and at 6:30 a.m., I fixed my feet properly on the nail board.

We were live on all the platforms. The timer began. It was go time.

Believe me when I say I had zero fear. I did my homework. It wasn't like it was back when I ran a forty-two-kilometer marathon with only fifteen kilometers of preparation. I was reckless back then. But with time and effort, you grow, learn, and become the person you dream of becoming. It's the time spent in the dark when no one is watching or looking. When it's you and only you during your cave days, paying the debt, making an effort, crying, screaming, and fighting the devil within, that's when you elevate.

I don't do any of this to show off or to prove anything to anyone. I'm only doing it to prove that I am who I am. I am the person I always dreamed of being. I am the person who will support my circle. I'm *ready* for setbacks, I'm ready for failure, I'm ready for pain, and I'll give my best and share love in this world until my last breath.

Love is the secret! I'm not talking about the love of attachment or the love of approval. No. Love is beyond that. Loving yourself with your flaws and with your past, loving your parents no matter how they raised you, loving your friends with zero expectations, and loving anyone and everyone. Love isn't something I do; it's something I become, and I love every bit of this existence. There are Auntie's words, "love life", and my motto, *Let's Live*. That's all there is.

For the first three hours, I was breathing and meditating. The sun was rising, and I only had piano music in my ears (Ludovico and Hans Zimmer).

At 10 a.m., some friends arrived. I was there physically, but mentally, I was somewhere else.

My sister-by-choice, Isabella, was the one getting my meals. She was always by my side in case I was thirsty, hungry, or needing something. I felt blessed for the people in my life.

Einstein said, "The body can go from point A to point B, but the mind can go anywhere."

At the five-hour mark, Zaher, who had traveled from Lebanon to be with me that day, made me listen to a voice note that Mom and Dad had sent to him. It touched me deeply. I was standing on the nails and started crying. "Why?" I guess it's love. I felt how much they loved me and were always by my side, even when they couldn't be physically with me. Their love was with me. I felt it.

While still standing on nails, I bent forward and cried like a baby, losing myself. Once I cried, the pain became non-existent. My crying had released serotonin and endorphins, and I actually felt high, as if I'd taken a certain pill to reduce the pain. The pain came in waves, but I accepted it. I didn't react to the pain. I took it in and let it flow through me.

Jhony and Ashraf, the two beasts, were handling all the filming, taking care of the live streaming, and actually producing the day.

Zaher, Jhony, Ashraf, and Isabella had made the day possible. Without them, it would've been impossible for me to accomplish the challenge. I'm blessed with the friends that I call family in my life.

At 1:00 p.m., I'd been standing for almost seven hours. We'd been live for those seven hours, with people interacting on social media and showing support.

My family in Lebanon were on their way to my auntie's funeral at that time. I was on the nail board in Dubai, my family at the funeral in Lebanon, and the other family at the funeral in Australia.

Life always surprises me.

People start to come by the location in Dubai. Some of them I knew, and some of them I didn't. Everyone was gathering and supporting. The energy was magical. I was standing like a tree, observing all that was happening. I was watching myself stand on nails, but I wasn't the one standing. I closed my eyes and drifted. I drifted into a moment where I became the moment. *Who am I?*

I am no one. I was a being having a human experience. My name, my religion, my color, and my race were non-existent. My auntie was in my heart. I felt my her. I felt her love. Love is beyond death. Love is a power that can never fade. I was dancing while my feet were stuck on the nail board. I was lost in the now, lost in tears, lost in smiles, lost within, and yet I'd found myself somewhere within myself.

At 4:00 p.m., I'd been standing for ten hours. I had a video call with Mom, surrounded by her family, after the funeral. Through all the pain of loss, I was there, standing for hope and inspired by love.

The garden was filled with fifty people sitting on the grass, watching me dance, cry, smile, and sing.

I felt the love of everyone. How did I feel it? At that moment, I couldn't feel the pain anymore. Waves of emotions passed by, and the energy of the place was glowing. I'm trying to describe in words what can't be described.

At 6:35 p.m., twelve hours had passed while I stood on the nail board.

I looked at Jhony and Zaher and said, "All set and done."

Everyone was around me as if we were one big family standing together. Love united us.

Ten, nine, eight, seven, six, five, four, three, two, one. The countdown for twelve hours, twelve minutes, and twelve seconds ended. My friends popped the confetti at zero, and Mom and my family were on a video call with us. Everyone was shouting and screaming, "Let's live," "Let's live, baby," "Woohoo!" Everyone was clapping. I wished I could hold on to this moment, but like every other moment, it passed by, leaving me with a feeling.

The next challenge was to remove my feet from the nail board. I sat on a chair and spent five minutes removing my right foot. Removing my foot after that long on the nails felt like I was removing a sword from my heart. There was one more foot left to remove. As soon as it was done, I knelt down, waiting for the excruciating pain.

There were twenty-five minutes of extreme pain. It felt like my feet were burning, but I couldn't do anything about the heat. I could only take it in.

As soon as my nervous system calmed down, I sat on the chair, thanking everyone for their support. I looked up to the sky and sent an intention: *I love you, Auntie*. I looked around and thought, *Life, I love you*.

YOUR LIFE IS IN YOUR HANDS

> "Your life is in your hands
> to make of it what you choose."

I don't want you to live my life, I don't want you to run marathons barefoot, I don't want you to stop partying, I don't want you to stop drinking, and I don't want you to become a monk or stand on nails for twelve hours. I want you to live with intention. That's it.

I'm sharing my life with you for you to know I was no one (and I still am). I was lazy, avoiding reality, delusional that I'd achieve my dreams, unhealthy, a burden on my family, and living life unconsciously.

But I paused for a while and asked myself, "Is this how I want to live?"

Even though I was doing what I love (magic), I was going in all directions. When I decided to become better, I made small adjustments to my life. Over a few years, life became bliss.

Remember this: The purpose of life is to live it and be happy, healthy, and strong.

Happiness isn't drugs. It isn't pills. Happiness is a state. If now, just right now, you say, "I'm grateful today that I'm alive," you're happy, my friend. It doesn't mean your debts are gone and the challenges perished. No. It means you're grateful to be alive. This in itself is happiness, and the rest you'll figure out. Be the light for the people around you, not the heavy weight. Be the hope, not the energy drainer, and be the love for anyone lost.

Ask me about health, as someone from whom it was stolen in a day. Every day, I had to go for a blood test before I started the day. I had to worry about the medications and listen to the doctor as they dictated my life with statistics and numbers. F**K NO! I don't want you to experience this. If you wake up sick, all your concerns will focus on how to feel okay. Run in the morning, fast for twelve hours, be aware of what you eat, be healthy, and enjoy the pleasurable stuff. In other words, balance your life.

You've seen how many times I cried in my life, and I still do. Every time I'm touched by life, I cry. I don't hold back. I know that I'm willing to do what I thought was impossible, especially for the people I love.

I'm ready for pain, for struggle, for sadness, and I'm ready for joy and bliss. I'm ready for whatever life has in store for me because I'm fully aware that no matter how strong I become, life will try to knock me down in the future. All I can do is be my best, be ready, and accept what's coming my way.

Being strong isn't just physical. Strong is letting go of what's holding you back. Strength is making the right decision, even when you're scared. Strength is taking responsibility for your actions.

Keep this in mind and understand that your mind will often convince you otherwise, but you know now you're not your mind. Take action, and you'll thank yourself in the future. Start easy. Start small. Small wins, every day. That's it!

I believe in this part of human evolution, a critical time in history. We must become better. We solved all the external problems in history—food, houses, travel, connection, transportation, and so on.

But we're living unconsciously. We hurt each other unintentionally. I was ignorant of how much stress I was causing my mom by being a dumb kid in school, with gambling, excessive drinking, and only caring about myself. I wanted to be happy and comfortable, regardless of anyone else.

It's time for all of us to shift inward and understand ourselves. People are angry about how there's no peace in the world. How do you think peace will be attained if we approach it angrily?

Be in tune with yourself, connect to yourself, and then you can connect to the world. Understand your flaws, and accept your mistakes. Learn to love yourself, and you'll be able to love the world. The number one reason I build a beautiful life is the support of the people around me. I'm indeed disciplined and the one who puts in the effort, but believe me, nothing would be possible if it wasn't for the beautiful people in my life.

When your friend needs your help, be there. When someone is talking to you, listen. Listen to what they're saying and understand what they mean. Whatever you want from life, give it first. Want to be successful? Financially? Spiritually? Whatever your definition of success is, start with caring about people.

Love doesn't mean not fighting for what you believe in. Instead, it's about standing for what you believe in.

Love is a power; there's no resistance against love. Hatred is a force that has resistance. Just look at the world. When people hate, other people hate them. But love? You can never fight love.

Human evolution is in my hands and your hands.

You may have noticed in my story that my initial plan isn't where I am now. Where we'll end up is something we don't know. All you need is a big goal—any big goal that makes sense to you—followed by the next step. If you believe in a creator but don't understand how life has been created, you're sure that it's here. Similarly, you'll never know exactly how to create your life; it will happen to you. Your part is to do your best. Pay in effort.

These realizations took me endless time, knowledge, discipline, and effort. You have to pay your dues, and you have to try to become one percent better every day. You have to build your life brick by brick, even if you were lucky enough to be born with a silver spoon in your mouth. Life isn't about money.

Life is about your experiences and how you share them with the world.

I saw myself as a successful person before anyone knew I existed. I was creating a to-do list every day and smashing it.

I promised myself something and kept my promise. Whenever I had an idea, I lived by it, documented it, edited it, posted it, and watched it by myself. Guess what?

Whenever I was done, I used to clap for myself.

When I started creating content, I wanted someone to film me, but it was a hassle. I did some magic shows and made some money, with which I bought my first camera. Then, I learned how to film myself.

I always asked someone to edit my videos, but it was irritating to not have control over it. So, I learned how to edit myself.

I was always copying someone else, and then I asked myself why I was doing it. I decided to create my own way.

While creating, sharing, and posting my ideas, I received minimal views, which was frustrating. I was reaching out to people with big numbers through DM and emails. But of course, they didn't reply. I remember saying to myself in 2020, "I'm not going to get anyone for me to get my voice out there. I'll do all I can."

I was waiting for something to happen, but then I realized it might or might not work. Then I realized no one cared about me and thought, *F**k it. I'll do it myself.*

Those videos where I was challenging myself every week are the reason for my success. I was short on cash, yet I promised myself I'd post one video weekly, so I started creating ways to challenge myself that wouldn't cost me money. I pushed myself daily, and they turned out to be physical and mental challenges that I learned so much from.

To be completely honest, running improved my life. To be able to set a physical goal and achieve it every day boosts your confidence and toughens your mind.

Running barefoot gave me the freedom to be who I wanted to be. Judge me however you want. I'd do my thing, focusing on myself and nothing else (more on this later).

So, what is the way? The way is putting effort into feeling alive. There is no other way.

The only real currency in life is effort. That's nature's law. You never plant a seed and give it money to grow. You have to prepare the soil, water it, take care of it, protect it, and be patient and consistent. And in one or two years, you'll get to eat the fruit.

TIME TO HARVEST THE FRUITS

"What you plant now, you will harvest later."

My family landed in Dubai on Thursday night, March 9, exactly one week after I set the world record for the longest duration of standing on nails for my auntie. After years of being a kid, reckless, broke, and sick, I was now renting my own apartment in Dubai with my own car. It sounds minimal, but it was the reward for my efforts.

I saved some money from previous shows, mentoring people online, helping others build a better life, and doing some advertising on Instagram.

Money will flow into your life when you're willing to sweat, work hard, and pay in effort.

For the first time in my thirty-one years, I was the one responsible for my family. I was the one taking care of them. I took them to the beach, took them out for dinner, took them shopping, took them to the zoo, and took them to a virtual reality arena. I bought Mom what she needed, got my sister what she wanted, and took care of Dad.

We used to wake up early, walk on the beach, and meditate together. I guided them on breathing, and Mom said, "I feel relaxed. I forgot what it means to be relaxed." It had been two years since her sister was first diagnosed, then cured, then received a terminal diagnosis, and eventually passed away.

I could only imagine the struggle she'd been through.

I did my best for them to have the best time, making sure to be around them twenty-four seven for those five days and listening to them.

People live abroad and send money to their parents. That isn't what they actually need. It's true that sometimes, financially supporting them is a must, but the truth is that they only want you to give them back the love and care you once needed when you were young.

I'm building my life so that no matter how busy I am, I'll have time for them to listen to their problems, talk with them, hug them, and tell them I love them while I can. Make this a daily reminder. Because one day, all this will be just a memory.

We had the best five days of our lives.

I'll take this moment to share some information with you about my life before January 8, 2017, which was the day I was diagnosed with blood cancer.

I was a turbulent kid in school, making noise and skipping classes. I was a pain in the ass. Mom always received calls from the school telling her that her son wasn't behaving. She never received a phone call that made her proud.

Growing up, when I was in university, I was neither a good guy nor a bad guy. I was transparent. I failed a semester, so my parents had to pay the tuition twice. I then grew up being a magician. They had always supported me, and I was making good money.

You know what's scary? I was in my early twenties, and a lot of money was flowing into my life. I was a good magician. I refined my skills, understood the game, and knew how to brand myself. I had plenty of free time, money in hand, and zero responsibilities.

I started clubbing every weekend, filling my free time, and aiming to pick up women and made that my purpose. In my mid-twenties, I started smoking pot (weed and hash). Eventually, I started gambling. First, I was playing $50 a night with friends. In no time, this $50 turned into $300, then $500, and then I was playing at the big tables. Once, I went to the casino and ended up losing $2,000 in a single night. Another night, I won $2,000. I was filled to the brim with a bad lifestyle, bad habits, and stress created by myself. I was hitting the gym, but it was for the sake of looking big, not to be healthy.

I was always honest with my parents. They knew about my gambling. They'd see me go out late and come back late, sleeping all day. Everything affected everything else. Cancer was my first reality check when I was twenty-five. But in a year, I recovered, and I was back to my old habits. I believed this was normal behavior; when you feel a part of your life was stolen from you, you go back to prove to yourself that you still have it.

When I turned twenty-eight, I wanted to do more. How? Earlier in the book, I mentioned starting with a morning routine of reading, running, and meditating. As soon as I had this mentality, I didn't have much time until COVID-19 hit. Living in Dubai is expensive; bills accumulate easily. I didn't get the chance to digest what was happening, and suddenly, I was one month behind on rent. Then another. I needed to buy my food and pay for my visa renewal. It was a domino effect. Soon enough, I was $10,000 in debt after just four months. Before the pandemic, I'd already started my self-discovery journey. To become better, I needed time.

The Lebanon crisis hit in mid-2020. Due to economic inflation, my parents' salaries lost ninety-five percent of their value. With each one making $2,000, inflation affected their salary to the point where it was only worth the equivalent of $200 a month for them. I was tight. I was broke. I couldn't do anything. They got to the point of saying, "This is too expensive. We can't buy it now." I was helpless.

■ ■ ■

Fast forward to Monday, March 13, 2023. Before dropping them to the airport for a flight to Lebanon, we were all having mate (yerba mate, a type of tea) together in the living room.

I was sitting in the middle of the sofa, hugging my mom on my right and my sister on my left while Dad was heating up the water.

Mom said, "You know, Ramy, with your history, I never expected that you'd ever make me proud. Gambling, drinking, chasing chicks, and not listening to us. I got to a point where I believed I made a mistake raising you. But now I'm grateful to have you as a son. I'm beyond proud that you're my son."

Mom was talking, and tears rolled down my cheek. I was at peace in a moment where nothing else could have made me feel the same. I thought running the marathon was the ultimate feeling, and then discovering the love of people on the nail board was the ultimate feeling. Then, I realized at that moment, on the couch in my living room, I was in the ultimate of the ultimates. Buddha calls this state "nirvana". No number, no achievement, no cars, and no drugs could even come close to what I felt. I was in a blissful state. It was another moment that I wished I could grasp.

Mom turned around, looked at my face, and asked, "Why are you crying?"

With a smile, I replied, "Life is amazing, Mom."

I was crying because of cave days, efforts put in, waking up early every day, and trying to become what I ought to be. Everyone doubted. Everyone thought I was losing my mind. Yet here I was. I was it. I'd become the person I once dreamed of becoming. With all the darkness that Mom had passed through, I was the light for her. I was the reason for her to look at life with hope after she lost her sister.

That's living, man. It's not pleasure or a smile or happiness. It's beyond that. It's peace.

Finally, it was time to harvest the fruits of my efforts.

PART 8

SLOWLY BUT SURELY

NEW ERA

"Life is not about receiving; life is about giving."

After the nail board challenge, I received DMs and messages from people who wanted to try the nail board, some who wanted to run with me, and others who wanted to know if I could mentor them regarding an issue they were facing. On my social platform, I announced that I'd be doing a Saturday morning meet and greet. We'd go for a light run, followed by a nail board session, and I'd discuss life with whoever would like to join. I had zero expectations of how many would attend.

In this age, we want to always take the easiest route. People want support, motivation, and help, but only through the easiest way. Only a few are the ones who push themselves. Please be one of those few, for your own sake.

On the first Saturday, there were five people, including me. Next Saturday, there were seven people. The following Saturday, eleven people gathered. The attendees loved gathering, connecting with others, and experimenting with pain.

Leave the gathering feeling good and feeling alive. That was my goal.

I searched for ways to improve, grow, and expand the meeting day.

I thought about how to explain life in a way for us to understand why we feel good sometimes and at other times we feel very low. This is the theory that explains it.

Theory of Neutralism

As an individual, you stand somewhere in the middle of the lifeline. The lifeline is straight but angled up by five degrees, and the line is soft, so you make a hole where you stand. Your brain creates a comfort zone around this state. You're not extremely happy or content in this state, but you're not sad or depressed. I call it the feeling-neutral zone. The only way to always feel good is to keep pushing beyond this comfort zone that minds create because, even if you stop, the line is angled slightly upward, and you're going to be moving slightly backward.

Once you keep pushing beyond this level through improvement, trying new experiences, growing in your career, and giving to others, you'll keep moving up the lifeline. But you must keep advancing outside your comfort zone—outside the neutral zone.

"Every life form seems to strive to its maximum except human beings. How tall will a tree grow? As tall as it possibly can."

This means there is only one way to live a good, meaningful life with a purpose. It's to constantly improve yourself, or you'll continue living in the neutral zone.

That is the secret to feeling good every day, living, not just existing, and truly feeling alive.

In a month, the word was out. I was posting videos about the event (it became an event), and we received at least thirty people each Saturday. The event was called *Let's Live Day*, followed by a theme.

The main theme was to *come and feel how good it is to be a human*. The day was a sample of my daily life, starting with a ten-minute talk, positive words, and affirmations. Then, there were ten to fifteen minutes of animal flow movement, followed by meditation and breathing, and an interactive exercise (such as eye gazing for two minutes with a person you just met today—very challenging, believe me). We wrapped up the day by standing on the nails, understanding pain in depth, and having an ice bath.

If you can imagine this for a moment, people arrive at our event dull, resistant, and skeptical about what the day will offer. They leave feeling elevated, happy, and fulfilled with the biggest smiles on their faces.

The power of these events isn't only about feeling good for one day. It's about opening a new thought pattern in your day, making you feel good—different from usual—and teaching you ways to feel good every day.

The day starts with your attendance but never ends with the day's closing. You have all your life to keep growing, evolving, and improving.

I also feel elevated during and at the end of these days. These events are the fuel for me to keep growing on a personal level because no matter how many messages I receive telling me that I inspire people (which I'm grateful for), meeting people in person and seeing them transform their lives, improve, tap in, and grow touches me on a deeper level. The events are growing, and the team is growing. My friends took part in the event, and we divided the tasks between us. Eventually, we reached an average of fifty people per event by the beginning of May.

I never looked at my competitors or anyone else doing similar activities. I wish the best for everyone. My concern was focused on how I could keep improving those days, how I could become better, how my friends and I could grow together, and how I could keep improving the quality of people's lives. That was it!

After three years of embracing the ideology of *Let's Live*, it's now finally clear in my head, and I can deliver the message to you easily. You'll actually feel alive if you attend and follow our guidelines in the events or you take five percent of the knowledge I share on social media or in this book.

This is *Let's Live*:

"Only by challenging yourself and being uncomfortable will you feel alive. Let's Live, baby! Woohoo!"

At the end of March 2023, I officially received the Guinness World Record for the longest duration (male) standing on a sadhu nail board. "Officially awesome" was written at the bottom of the certificate. I have a certificate for being awesome.

I never stopped working on myself while my life was expanding. I was running every day, reading, meditating, experimenting with ice baths, and stretching my mind and body. My morning routine is sacred; it's where I built myself. It's my zone. It's where I assess my life, reflect, and make big decisions.

At the end of May, it was time to go to Lebanon for the summer. I'd been reflecting on how I wanted to approach that summer in Lebanon, and I had great ideas for the summer, but before we get to that, I want to share a story with you.

The Chef Who Changed His Life

Six months after accomplishing my first barefoot marathon, I was in Buddha-Bar Dubai. Isabella, the GM and my sister-by-choice, was the one who took care of my meals when I was setting a world record on the nail board. We were having a cup of coffee together. She mentioned that the chef of Buddha-Bar, Alex, would like to meet me.

I love meeting people and hearing their stories.

As soon as he arrived, I stood up, we shook hands, and he said, "I was one hundred and twenty-one kilograms at the end of 2022, and I felt heaviness in my chest, so my colleague took me to the emergency room." I stood and listened, not saying a word. He continued, "I had high blood pressure and high cholesterol, and ninety percent of my arteries were blocked. I was that close to dying of a heart attack."

He indicated a small gap using his thumb and index finger.

I looked at him. He was in his mid-thirties. This wasn't normal for a man his age.

"The doctor gave me two options. One was to pop a bunch of pills and have heart surgery. The other was to change my life."

I nodded, knowing how the first option usually ends—more complications and more pills.

"The second option was to change my life, how I eat, diet, move, and think. Basically, my entire lifestyle."

I'm honestly glad that the doctor gave him the second option.

"I saw your videos running, and also watched your marathon barefoot and said to myself, 'If this guy can run forty-two kilometers barefoot, I'm sure I can run ten minutes with shoes'," Alex said.

Those moments are the moments that I live for—the goosebumps.

"Wow, what an amazing initiative," I said.

I'm really surprised and astonished at how he made such a decision. It's not easy for someone who's one hundred and twenty-one kilograms to do that.

"I know it's going to take time, but I'll get there," Alex said.

"Indeed, slowly but surely," I responded.

"Today I'm one hundred kilograms. I lost twenty-one kilograms in the past six months, and my blood pressure and cholesterol levels are back to normal. My arteries improved by sixty percent," Alex said.

Fired up, I said, "F**k yeah, baby!"

"I've never felt that good in my life. I want to thank you."

"Thank yourself, bro. You're the one putting in the effort. I'm the one who showed you that effort is the way. Nothing more," I said.

We hugged, and I said, "I'm so proud of the effort you are making, bro! And thank you for sharing your story with me."

All you need is one good decision, and your life will change. Success is becoming who you always dreamed of being.

4 WHYS

"The road map for the good life."

First: Why Run?

Running has endless physical benefits. It improves blood circulation to your lungs, heart, and other organs and boosts your immune system. We all learned this when we were in school.

But running also makes you a better human. Here is why:

- Running is a physical challenge. You need to train your mind to accomplish physical challenges. There are times when your mind tells you to stop, but you keep pushing to achieve the goal. It's a skill that's required in all aspects of life. It's where you connect with the devil within.
- Running is one of the hardest physical challenges. It requires a good aerobic base, endurance, focus, and being with yourself.

- Running affects the brain. A brain image study by David Raichle at the University of Arizona showed clear differences in the brain activity of serious runners compared to well-matched non-runners. They studied the two different brains. For the runner, they saw increased coordinated activity in regions, mainly at the front of the brain, known to be involved in executive function and working memory. Second, they saw a relative dampening of activity in the default mode network, a series of linked brain regions that spring into action whenever we're idle or distracted. Individuals with major depressive disorder showed increased or decreased default mode network activity relative to controls. In other words, running affects the default mode network, causing it to drop, which, if elevated, can cause depression.
- Running improves aspects of executive function, as shown in a study by a Lithuanian sports university. Executive function is the ability to marshal attention, tune out distractions, switch between tasks, and solve problems.
- The hippocampus—the part of the brain associated with memory and learning—has been found to increase in volume in the brains of regular runners.
- Running heals the brain. The body and mind keep the score for every trauma or negative emotion you experience. Because of its positive impact on the mind/body spectrum, running heals you.

Can you believe the benefits of this simple act of just making the body move in its simplest form?

My Flatmate Steve's Story

I call him Steve here for privacy reasons.

Steve came to Dubai looking for a new chapter of his life and was scared about the future. Steve was filled with fear and insecurities and was worried about being a failure. He never challenged himself.

He took a job in Jordan for a year, but wasn't content with the job or the lifestyle. He then went back to Lebanon. He started another job in Lebanon but was still not satisfied. He applied for a job in Dubai and received a job offer, but doubted his ability to make the right decision and worried about the logistics of moving out of Lebanon again. He questioned himself constantly, wondering where to live, what would happen if he failed again, and what would happen if he couldn't keep the job.

He reached out to me through my DMs and asked for a mentorship. At that time, I was giving Lebanese people free mentorship sessions to support them. We jumped on a call, and Steve shared the salary and his concerns with me. I told him that getting out of your comfort zone is always the best option, and when he asked questions regarding where to live, I said, "I have a guest room, I keep it for guests visiting. You can use it for at least the first month while you figure out your life."

Steve signed his contract three days after the call, and six days after our call, he was living at my place.

His goal was to become better. The first words I said to Steve were, "Let's run," and off we went.

He started waking up early, joining me on my runs, reading from my library, and writing down his goals.

I advised him, "If you want to become better, keep running with me." I taught him how to breathe while running, how to stretch after the run, and how to improve. Slowly but surely.

In two months, he was able to run a marathon. He was performing as one of the top three in his job. The company's CEO had a talk with him, telling him that the company's best decision was when it hired him.

If you met Steve when he moved to Dubai, and met him again now, you wouldn't recognize him as the same person. And running is what made him improve. Of course, he was putting in the work, but running was the foundation. Imagine—he ran for his life, and his life improved.

By the way, we became family, and he's part of *Let's Live*.

Based on my experience and knowledge to the day I'm writing this book, I believe that running barefoot has even more benefits than the one described. One of them is the ability to focus. My prefrontal cortex, the area of the brain handling focus, is highly activated during my barefoot run. My brain is fully aware of what is on the ground, so I don't step on glass, tiny rocks, or anything that might hurt my feet.

Also, my body has discharged itself from all the negative emotions since I started running barefoot. I feel good ninety-five percent of the time. I'm aware that I changed my life in a way to ensure I feel good every day, but running is a big part of it.

I can't prove it scientifically yet. Hopefully, I can in the future, but this is my discovery, and my conclusions are based on my experimentations.

Go ahead! Go for your first run, with or without shoes, or a slow jog. Don't hurt yourself, and don't go for a sprint right away. Take it slow and easy. I'm with you. And if you feel like sharing your run, feel free to tag me: *@ramynaouss*.

Second: Why Breathe and Meditate?

Breathing

Breathe properly because it's a medicine that no one taught us how to use. Breathing should always be from the nose. While working out, inhalation can be from the nose and exhalation from the mouth. Occasionally, inhale and exhale from the mouth only for high-intensity exercise or a specific breathing technique.

Breathing from the mouth has immense negative effects. The air that reaches the lungs isn't filtered. When breathing from the mouth, the mind-body thinks you're in flight-or-fight mode, which leads to high cortisol levels. This is the number one reason for stress and anxiety.

Once you take a slow, deep breath from the nose and exhale from the mouth, you enter a relaxed state.

Try it now. Take a breath from your nose while counting to three and exhale from the mouth while counting to six. Do it ten times and see how relaxed you feel. *Tekram* (this is the Lebanese word for welcome).

Meditation

Meditation has endless benefits for the brain. Endless.

It affects the brain similarly to running in many aspects. You can re-read what I wrote about the benefits of running. No joke.

Additionally, meditation is being mindful. Mindfulness is the act of being aware of your thoughts and body and what you're sensing and feeling at that moment. It's about being present.

Meditation blocks all the outer distractions and takes you to your inner world. You shouldn't control anything while meditating other than slowing your breathing. There's nothing to expect. A major misconception is that you should feel a certain way when meditating. You don't have to feel anything. You just have to learn to watch your thoughts, not control them, and watch without reacting. This is where you start learning to detach from your thoughts and emotions.

It's important to note that meditating only once won't give you the benefits you seek. You start feeling calmer when you continuously do it for at least five minutes over at least ten days. This is crucial.

Third: Why Read?

Thank you for taking the time to read my book. Reading changed my life for a reason. I listened to people who achieved their dreams, created a good life, and gave positive reinforcements every day. I was surrounded by people whom I looked up to. That was the only way I could be with them. When everyone around me was nagging, complaining, talking about how life isn't fair to them, and gossiping, I was reading about big entrepreneurs who made it happen, studies and science about the brain, psychology, history, religion, and even daily information that stretched my mind. Reading about positivity—the example of how your life perspective will change if you keep looking at the glass as half full—was where I built my new philosophy about life.

The problem with change isn't that it's impossible. It's because of our beliefs that change is impossible. So, change your beliefs, and change will become possible.

Fourth: Why Challenge Yourself?

Nothing in life taught me more about myself than challenging myself did. Before the big challenges, I started with minor ones.

I don't like hikes. I tried them, and I discovered something new.

I don't like to do yoga. I pushed myself to attend a yoga class, and I learned something new.

I don't know how to film and edit. I spent two years filming and editing every day. This was how my videos with my ideas became viral.

I'm scared of heights. I went and became a skydiver. You know how much I pushed myself and doubted this step. Yet, when I accomplished my first few jumps, I felt I was unstoppable.

Every step is one step on the ladder of success.

After those challenges, I didn't have enough money to do other activities. So, I created ways to challenge myself with zero costs. That in itself was a challenge to push my creativity.

Only by pushing yourself outside your comfort zone will you meet yourself and feel good about yourself.

You know the people who challenge themselves and push to come to one of our events? How good and powerful they feel after the events? It's challenging to go to an event where you have no idea what will happen.

These four whys are the number one reason for success. You need to be mentally strong, and your brain must be sharp (running). You need to be calm and see through any hardship that comes your way, plus assess your previous moves (meditate and breathe). You need to have knowledge, inspiration, and ideas about improving and becoming better (read). You need to be ready to be uncomfortable often to grow (challenge yourself).

These are the secrets, but they need effort, consistency, perseverance, discipline, and patience to change your life. It's all in your hands.

PART 9

LIVE LIFE

HOW WOULD YOU KNOW IF YOU DON'T TRY?

"Life is a philosophy. Create your own."

When I started running barefoot, I wanted to heal my knee and back. But that wasn't enough. I've always wondered if running barefoot could help my body recover from cancer (science is revealing the major benefits of grounding and earthing) or *maybe* even prevent it. Every experience I delved into was checking how my body could be in its best shape (looking good and feeling great).

That's the reason I started fasting in the first place. That's why I went for six months without processed sugar and avoided processed food. That's why I learned so much about food and diets. That's why I explored and studied breath, the gut, and the brain (mostly individual research). That's why I started running in the first place.

My number one purpose in life after my diagnosis was to figure out how to let my body heal itself. The other was how I could reach the best version of myself mentally, overcome my mind, and be more and do more for this world.

The two ideologies supported each other, and they still do. They were ignited by the idea of overcoming the disease and maybe discovering ways for other patients to overcome their cancer and designing a way for people to create a good, healthy, and strong life for themselves.

Now, scientists and doctors are discussing and proving how being barefoot reduces inflammation in the body, enables better circulation, and helps the body discharge negative energy. I'm already two years ahead in experimenting. I'm winning either way. If I discover a revelation about being barefoot, it's one big point to me. If not, it was fun trying, at least. The world is concerned about wellbeing, yet it's very easy nowadays to forget ourselves.

My ideology and philosophy was, is, and will always be, *Let's Live.*

Take advice but not orders. Listen to everyone, but then think, study, and come up with your own conclusion. Never assume before trying. Never judge. Share your opinion only when you have all the inputs and have experimented with it yourself. Keep an open mind about life. What is wrong is obvious. Don't kill. Don't steal. Don't hate. Don't hurt. Be loyal. We all know these rules, but I'll add to them.

Never think you're right and the person in front is wrong. Listen to their opinion, try to understand, then share your opinion. Arguing is a waste of time, and exchanging information is a form of enlightenment.

There's no reality in life. There's only perception. Maybe one day, when we die, we actually wake up from a dream in another dimension. Maybe we reincarnate. Maybe it's the end. Maybe we'll meet God. How would you know if you didn't try?

Is there a God? We pray with our hands open, looking to the sky as if God is up there. But imagine if the earth was upside-down in the moment of your prayers, so it meant you were directing your prayers downward, not to Him …

We can never understand what God is. If there's a creator of this life, we barely understand it. How can we even understand the creator of what we barely understand? Yet God manifests in nature. I learn from nature. If you plant the seed, take care of it, and put in effort, you'll harvest the fruit. This is the lesson I follow to reach God. I put in effort and give with no expectations. It's called love. So, I concluded God is love.

Is there a higher power? I reached places where I felt there was a power carrying me—a power lifting me. Can I prove it? No. Can I argue with you if you disagree? No. Based on my experience, I concluded there might be a higher power, and maybe this higher power is God.

Is there one way of living life? No. Live it the way it makes sense for you. What's for sure is that you must do good and be good. This is our human purpose. Eventually, it will come back to you. We're spiritual beings having a human experience. Get lost in this experience.

Is running barefoot the secret to a good life? Not necessarily. But running is the secret of a good life. It's one aspect of how I created a good life for myself, and I love it. I also taught people how to run, and they changed their lives.

Story of Dani

Dani (name changed for privacy) is an old friend of mine who lives in Lebanon. We were close when we were teenagers. Growing up, I got busy with my life. He got busy with his.

I saw him a few times over the past five years on big occasions, such as weddings and concerts, while I was fully focused on getting better, evolving, and improving. He got lost along the way. Believe me, he had all the reasons to do so. Pandemic, economic crisis, heartbreak, negativity around, toxic workplace, and being broke. Life actually gets really tough sometimes. And it did for him.

He contacted me in May 2023, saying, "I'm sick of my life." He'd been doing drugs on and off for the past four years. He tried ending it all a couple of times, yet always went back. He made an effort to stop drugs and switched to alcohol. He got to a point where he lost hope of recovering.

I replied to him, "I promise you, this will change this summer. On one condition."

"Whatever it is, I'm ready," Dani said.

"I'm coming back to Lebanon next month. Get ready."

When I was back in Lebanon, I made him jump in an ice bath and stand on a nail bed. You can never stop a bad habit unless you get a similar feeling somewhere else.

Let me explain. While doing drugs, you get a high. A dopamine rush. Whenever you want to stop taking drugs, your brain becomes hungry for that rush. If you don't get dopamine from somewhere else, you're always going to snap back.

Standing on a nail board releases endorphins because of the pain, making you feel good, calm, and relaxed. Ice baths release dopamine, a chemical that makes you feel content and happy naturally. These things were much-needed in his case.

Dani and I ensured this was a daily ritual he needed to begin with. You can never change unless you start feeling good about yourself. But a brain used to drugs and alcohol is a damaged brain. How else could I support him to heal his brain? Running.

In the next phase, which is after two days, I asked him to run for ten minutes. He'd never run before. He had zero clue about how to run. He struggled, barely accomplishing two kilometers without coughing, sweating, and chest pain (he was a heavy smoker).

The next day, he did it again. But this time, I advised him to breathe deeply and focus on his breath.

He slowly started getting better. Scientific studies that were shared previously in this book show how much running improves the brain. For example, a 2018 experiment from West Michigan University showed that running quickly for half an hour improves "cortical flicker frequency". Yet I personally believe running recovers, heals, and elevates the brain.

I only shared with him the guidelines I'm sharing with you. The rest was based on his efforts. Slowly but surely, he was getting better, feeling better, and becoming better.

For the first two months, he was completely sober. He relapsed once on alcohol, but woke up the second day straight away for a run.

Here's the most beautiful part; I have goosebumps as I'm writing this. Six months in, Dani was completely sober (the devil took over his mind for only two nights, and he drank, but the next day, he was back in the zone). He got a job offer in Dubai and ran a marathon. He's now a part of *Let's Live*. He started reading and taking back control of his life.

Keep in mind that he still has a lot of work to do, and reflect on where he started and how he turned into a different person today.

Unfortunately, my friend, there's no way in this life except to push through pain and put in the effort.

Will running change your life? Will challenging yourself change your life? Will meditation make you better? How would you know if you never tried?

OUTWITTING THE DEVIL

"The outer work can never be small if the inner work is
great. And the outer work can never be great
if the inner work is small."

I landed in Lebanon on Friday, June 16, at 11:00 a.m. and immediately headed home for lunch with the family. When I was still in Dubai the week before, I ran my second marathon. I woke up on a Saturday; my two flatmates and I were organizing ourselves for the marathon. Two of us were running and the other was handling the fueling for us. I beat my personal record that I'd set during the first marathon.

First marathon barefoot: five hours, forty-two minutes, and twenty-eight seconds.

Second marathon barefoot: three hours, fifty-nine minutes, and forty-two seconds.

My goal was to reach the end before four hours, and I finished with eighteen seconds to spare.

Driving back from the airport, gazing outside the car window, I was excited for the next day. Every summer in Lebanon seems like a new chapter. Lebanon is different from Dubai. Dubai is mainly flat, while Lebanon has many hills—ups and downs. Dubai streets are smooth, while Lebanon's asphalt is rough. The next day, I was on the street, hitting my first ten kilometers. The weather was beautiful. Life was good.

I was experimenting with the weather, the asphalt, the streets, and the hills. After a week of casual runs, I sat on my chair in the garden in my Zen space, wondering if I wanted to enjoy running in Lebanon. I thought maybe I should try running long distances there.

I had to create a system to make it fun. A system where I could challenge and stretch myself, not just make it a workout. Remember? Running is a lifestyle, not a workout. Thinking of it this way is the only way I can keep improving and still love it.

If I was a person who runs on a treadmill, you'd have never heard of me. It's lame and boring.

The first idea I had was to run to my cousin's house. Later, he could drop me back home. I was living in Zalka. He lived in Broumana. It was slightly farther than ten kilometers to run there. It sounded fun! I called him right then, even though it was nighttime.

"Hey, Couz! Tomorrow, I'm coming over for a cup of coffee in the morning," I said.

"What time?" he asked.

"7:30 a.m."

This is why my cousin hates me. All my plans start early, while his mornings begin at 10:00 a.m.

The next day, I woke up at 5:30 a.m., warmed up a bit, and at 6:00 a.m., I began running to his place. The road is a constant uphill climb. I was on the first four kilometers, and it began to get to me. I continued with a minute of running, followed by a minute of fast walking. My heart rate was above 160 all the way (60–80 beats per minute is the resting heart rate, and it increases to 120–140 when you work out; above 140 is considered intensive). I finally reached my cousin's place in one hour and seventeen minutes. The best part was the last bit, which was downhill, so I finished with a sprint.

When running in the morning on an empty stomach and finishing with a sprint, your brain shuts off completely. You enter an altered conscious state.

My vision and perspective changed. Everything I saw became vibrant. I saw life in everything around me. The colors were more vivid. Trust me, it's better than any pill, powder, or herbs I have tried.

When I arrived at my cousin's place, he, my auntie, and I sat in the garden. I was high on life after the run, feeling extra. My auntie came out with a bowl of fruits—watermelon (my favorite), apple, and peach. I was tasting heaven. Running made me appreciate the small things, such as drinking water and eating refreshing fruits.

Around 9:00 a.m., it was time for me to go back. I thought, "Why not run back home?"

As soon as I had the thought, the devil tried to convince me otherwise. "No need, man! You ran more than ten kilometers today. Why struggle?"

By now, you know me well. I don't listen to the devil. I told my cousin that I'd be running back.

"Bro, I can drop you off," my cousin said.

"I feel like running back home."

"You sure?" he asked.

"I'm never sure. But I feel it."

He agreed. I hugged him, thanked my auntie, and started my way back.

I was intrigued by the idea of, "What if I run back home? How would I feel?"

Historically, we humans used to walk and run to meet friends living in another village. So why not in 2023? Shouldn't I live primally?

In the summer of 2023, when all sorts of transportation were available, I picked the most challenging one. I ran to my cousin's home to visit him, then I ran back home. I reached home after an hour and two minutes, since the way back was mainly downhill.

As soon as I got home, I felt ecstatic. I wasn't sure what the right word was, but I was feeling … "Wow!"

This run was one of the decisions that would affect all my future decisions. I knew it from the moment it happened because this achievement was between me and myself. No one really cared about it except me. That is why this accomplishment touched me. I was lost within, which is how I found and stretched myself.

Every experience you endure has a positive or negative feeling linked to it. Going to the beach with your friends is connected to a positive feeling, which is why you're prone to repeat this experience.

Yet when you work out, run, or undertake any sort of challenging experience, you feel pain, nausea, and shortness of breath, so you struggle. This is because you're linking this experience to a negative one, and that's why you're most likely not going to repeat it.

But here's the secret: Once you learn to attach a positive feeling to a challenging and painful experience, you become superhuman.

When I push through a physical challenge, I accept the pain while in the process until the challenge is accomplished. I memorize the good and positive feeling of accomplishment, and the memory of the pain subsides. That's my secret of how I can push and face bigger and harder challenges.

For you, my friend, I offer this simple tip: Once you push yourself, the secret isn't to make it so hard that the scale of pain is way above the sense of accomplishment.

Take running as an example. If your best was five kilometers, you'd struggle to accomplish a half marathon (the scale of pain and struggle is way above the sense of accomplishment). You're most likely going to avoid running a half marathon again. But if you pushed for eight or ten kilometers, it would be a decent challenge. You'd struggle for a bit, but when you finished, the sense of accomplishment and positive reward would be greater than the negative feeling.

Another example is hiking. If you usually hike four kilometers at a slow pace, going on an extremely long hike of sixteen kilometers with pain and struggle would be way above the positive reward.

I'm not saying this is the only right way to do it, but when I did my first marathon barefoot, I didn't enjoy the experience. I faced a great deal of pain and struggle. It took me almost ten months to run a marathon again. I love running. But I could have easily let go of running if I didn't know how to smoothly install it back in my life.

When you aim to start waking up early, the same principle applies. If you usually wake up at noon, it will be challenging to start waking up at 5:00 a.m. A good place to start would be 11:00 a.m., then you'd gradually move it further back.

This is why the best motto to stick by is "slowly but surely".

The run to my cousin's home changed the direction of my summer in Lebanon. Every week, on my long runs, I ran to a destination. I had a motive for the run. The goal wasn't simply the run itself. One day, I ran eight kilometers to reach a friend. We ran five kilometers together, enjoyed some fruits, and I ran eight kilometers back.

Another day, I went with Mom to her office. We spent beautiful quality time on the road in the morning. She arrived at her office. I hugged her, reminded her to have a great day, and told her I love her so much. Then, I ran eleven kilometers back home.

I found a way to incorporate running long distances into my life in a way that wasn't about discipline anymore. It was love. I love running in the morning when it's peaceful. I love spending time with people I admire and enjoying the greenery of Lebanon and the good weather.

Believe me, *love is the way.*

Eventually, scouts, corporates, and villages were inviting me to speak at their events, gatherings, and meetups. This was another way to run to different locations.

On Thursday, July 27, 2023, I'd been in Lebanon, running uphill for over a month. I'm better at running uphill than downhill. I had a speech with a scout at 2:00 p.m. It was midsummer, and the weather was really hot, around 35 °C. The distance to reach was twenty-five kilometers uphill at an elevation of 1,058 meters.

I began my journey from home at 10:00 a.m. (Mom was going to meet me later at the location to drive me back.) The first ten kilometers were easy. My heart rate was 150–155 bpm. Perfect.

Around 11:30 a.m., I was on my thirteenth kilometer. The asphalt began to heat up, and my feet started to burn. I entered an altered conscious state, fully present. My only concern became to run to the next shade, stay hydrated, and keep moving. In this state, I was fully aware of myself. Nothing beyond the present existed. The devil showed up on my shoulder. "Call a taxi." "Ask a friend." "Call your mom to pick you up." I ignored all his words.

The more I pushed, the warmer the weather got. The asphalt was really boiling. I had one purpose, and it was to reach the destination. I accepted the pain in my feet and the struggle my body was going through and kept my focus.

In these moments, I'm not Ramy. I dissolve. All my identities disappear. I become an animal, hunting for the goal. It's as if I snap out of the reality of how to behave, talk, and walk. I become lost between the mountains, within myself. This is where I meet my true self.

I reached the location at 2:08 p.m. after running for four hours. All the struggles and the pain perished, and a sense of ultimate high took over me.

You've noticed in this book how passionately I talk about running. Running isn't a workout just to be healthy. It's beyond that.

Here is what running is.

Running long distances is underrated. Every long run is a trip to my inner world. It's quality time with my dark side. There's a voice that I only hear after fifteen kilometers of a long run when I'm drenched in sweat and covered in soreness. That voice has no filter. The devil's voice, the devil within, speaks to me loud and clear. It tries to convince me to stop, bail, and not reach the goal, and I have one option. I keep running and nothing else.

In this state, I become an animal, a machine. This mental chatter plagues most people out of their true potential. Action is the only state that exists at this moment: the next step, the next stride, the next kilometer, and the next breath.

I built my mental toughness by spending enough time with that voice when the devil was on my shoulder while pushing myself to accomplish the task. This mental toughness is what I need in every aspect of my life—every time I needed to improve a habit, every time I needed to make a big decision, and every time I needed to close a big business deal.

This is why I run. I want to become a better human and becoming better involves dealing with the inner devil. This devil is the reason for sadness, guilt, shame, regret, hurt, wars, envy, fear, comparison, racism, desire, grief, and apathy.

And the high state of consciousness (or altered conscious states) that I attain, by whatever means, is experiencing my inner reality. Most people are so detached from their own states of pure consciousness that they don't recognize themselves when they experience it because their identity with their lower ego and a negative self-image blot out the joy and bliss of life.

It's when reaching a higher self that high states of consciousness can be attained through long runs (I think barefoot is one of the reasons—I'm not sure, though, since I never ran long distances with shoes on), ice baths, constant nail board practice, and experiencing *samadhi* through meditation, daily breathwork, classical music, and art, or through the practice of spiritual disciplines.

Some thoughts in retrospect ...

Feed a lion until he's full, then let a prey pass by. He won't flinch. But let the lion be hungry, and he'll transform into the scariest, strongest, and most ferocious species on Earth.

Apply the same principle to a human. Place plenty of food on his plate, require zero effort, and entertain him with his comforts (TV, phone, gadgets), and this human will become the laziest, weakest, and sickest of all.

Yet, place this same human in tough conditions, make him hungry, and you'll see what he can do. This human will become stronger and smarter and will use all his strength.

Fun fact: Humans are the only species that can be hungry for things other than food. They're hungry for a goal, hungry to protect their family, and hungry to step out of a bad situation.

This is the main reason I'm always pushing myself in my runs, in my meditations, on the nail board, in the ice baths, and in my fasting. This is how I keep elevating, discovering myself, and reaching a high-level human status.

While spending the summer in Lebanon, the idea of running an ultramarathon barefoot floated in my brain. With every long run, I was testing my potential and testing the fueling (it's very important to eat while running long distances).

My friends and I formed a group of five that ran long distances together every Sunday. I was also loading a long distance midweek, averaging sixty-five kilometers per week. It's fun to run with friends, even though the time is spent running, not talking. It feels good.

Every Sunday, I woke up between 4:30 and 5:00 a.m. Two years back, I was sleeping at that time. It's beautiful how life can change when you change.

This summer consisted of long runs, meditations, reading, filming content, and expanding *Let's Live* while doing an event every

Saturday and spending quality time with my family and friends. It was that simple, but I loved every bit of it.

At the end of July, I aimed to run a marathon but had to stop at the thirty-six-kilometer mark because my body was extremely dehydrated. I felt very dizzy while running, and I had to stop.

I recovered mid-week, and the issue was fixed. I returned the first Sunday of August and hit my third marathon, though as it was a humid day, I couldn't break my personal record. I finished this marathon in four hours and six minutes.

My body felt great when I accomplished the third marathon, and I knew I could push further. I decided this with a close friend, who also happens to be my physiotherapist and bio-mechanic, Joseph Bahre. I love how humble he is. He goes on barefoot runs to understand the mechanics of running barefoot in depth so he can guide and advise me better.

During mid-August, I hit my first fifty-kilometer barefoot run, finishing light and easy. A few days later, I released the video announcing my sixty-three-kilometer run on September 10.

I picked almost the same trajectory as the previous year (my first marathon barefoot), and I added twenty-one kilometers before the starting point of the previous year's twenty-one kilometers.

The run had three purposes:

- I was eager to test myself after a year.

- "Run for love." Last year, 2023, was one of the hardest years. I started the year with just enough money to live during the first month. I lost my auntie, which affected Mom badly. A girl I loved, who I thought would be my partner, left me cold on a random day. Yet, I made that year one of the best years of my life for one reason: I love life.
- When I decided to run sixty-three kilometers, I felt scared (which is normal whenever you leave your comfort zone). I wanted to take a leap in my runs because when I returned to Dubai, I'd be taking a big leap with my decisions and personal goals. Running sixty-three kilometers is similar to the entrepreneurial challenges I'd face in Dubai.

I accomplished the sixty-three kilometers, which meant I'd accomplished my goals that season.

On Sunday, September 10, I woke up at 3:00 a.m. By 3:30 a.m., my friends and I were heading to the starting point in Raouche in the heart of Beirut. At 3:50 a.m., I hugged Mom, Dad, and my sister. I then began my run. There were almost fifty people by my side. Mom was driving behind me, Dad was running by my side, my best friend Zaher was in the car in front of me, and other friends were driving by my side. Feels like déjà vu, right?

It felt magical. Running brings people together. Instead of being separated by our ego minds, we become united in motion.

The first ten kilometers were a warm-up. During the second ten kilometers, I was keeping the rhythm. My pace was six minutes and fifty seconds per kilometer. During the third ten-kilometer section, the sun was rising, and so was my excitement as to what was next. People were switching roles and taking rests, then running again.

What was special about this run was that we shared the trajectory online with the estimated time at each point. Amazing people were joining, running alongside me. It touched my heart.

At the forty-kilometer mark, it was around 8:00 a.m. I started to feel the rays of the sun. I was still feeling fine, though, thanks to my efforts the previous year.

Running a marathon wasn't a challenge anymore. I grew, and I elevated. So, after the fifty-kilometer mark, the actual challenge began. I entered the dark zone (I'd never pushed to this level). But this time, I was ready.

At the fifty-second kilometer, the only problem I was facing was the heat. My body was already heated from running for more than five hours. There was nothing for as far as I could see, just like how when your phone overheats, it stops functioning until it cools down.

I was heating up, but I didn't want to stop. I was hunting for the goal. I asked the fueling car to keep cold water available.

During the fifty-third kilometer, I felt dizzy and nauseous. My gut wasn't accepting the fuel. The devil showed up. "It is time to stop." "You won't finish it." "If you keep running, you'll faint." Believe me, everything he said was valid. I actually thought I was going to faint at some point. In this state, I turned all my focus within, shifted to heavy breathing, let go of all those ideas, and pushed for the next kilometer. I took it one kilometer at a time. I slowed my pace to seven minutes and fifteen seconds per kilometer, dropped cold water on my head, and kept going.

"It's not about winning. It's about finishing." That was what I was telling myself. I stayed in this zone from fifty-three kilometers until fifty-nine kilometers, until I said to the devil, "I'm ready to die. If I'm not dead yet, I'll keep going."

This sentence revealed an inner beast I never knew I had. I accepted the pain, the discomfort, and the dizziness. Once I accepted those feelings, they perished.

I entered the sixty-kilometer mark. I was good, man. Really good. I had goosebumps and beautiful people by my side. I wasn't running. I was hopping like a gazelle as if I'd just started running. With every stride, I was clapping and screaming, saying:

"*Oum ya ensen!*" (Rise, you human!)

"*Fekrak hame iza 3:00 a.m. berkuud haffe walla la2, lek l 3alam chou helwe, leik l hayet chou helwe*" (Do you think I care if I'm barefoot or not? Look at the beautiful people surrounding me. Look how beautiful life is.)

"*Oum chouf ade awe tkoun ensen.*" (Rise and see how powerful it is to be a human.)

Similar to the previous year, the municipality of Batroun had prepared a tent as the finish line for us. I loved and appreciated their constant support. A lot of people gathered around the tent for our arrival.

I finally entered the tent (finish line).

I WATCHED MY OWN FUNERAL

"Life is not about having; it is about letting go."

I sat on the floor, taking a few breaths to return to reality. After running for seven hours, the body needs time to recalibrate and find balance. My vision was mellow, seeing life in all things and feeling the asphalt moving beneath me. Yet there were no tears. Instead, I was smiling. Mom was smiling. Even though the tent was crowded, I felt at peace. We took some pictures, drank special lemonade, thanked everyone, and we were on our way back home.

Another memory stuck in the depths of my soul.

You can watch the full video of the run and the story behind it on my YouTube channel: *@ramynaouss*. The video is called *I Ran 1,358 km Barefoot to Discover This*.

To answer some questions going through your head:

- Yes, there was a time during the run when I felt as if I was watching myself running, and I wasn't the one running. I've been reaching this state often in my long runs.
- Yes, I was in an altered conscious state above forty kilometers. Fully present. It's true that it was covered with dizziness and nausea, but it was f**king amazing to be in an elevated state around people I love and their energies.
- Of course, my feet were hurting. I ran sixty-three kilometers on rough asphalt. "It doesn't get easy, man. You just get stronger."
- Yes, running is a drug. It elevates me. I get high while running, my skin glows, my brain upgrades, my senses are better, and my feelings are enhanced.

A couple of days after September 11, 2023, I woke up on a Thursday, walked straight to my laptop, and started watching all the footage again. I prepared a cup of yerba mate, sat in my garden, took a few slow breaths, closed my eyes, and started to meditate.

The same question had been running through my brain for the last few days, *Why was I crying endlessly last year when I reached the finish line?*

I didn't react to the thought. I stayed still, giving my brain some time to connect the dots. We humans have all the answers within. It's mentioned through all religions, and following some tips of this book, you can find your answers. You must sit in peace and close your eyes. Some call it praying, others meditation. Whatever you want to call it, the method is simple. Sit in silence and close your eyes. Do it every day with zero expectations. That's it.

■ ■ ■

Let me take a moment and explain how to meditate.

Sit and take a deep breath. Inhale from the nose for three seconds and exhale from the mouth for six seconds. Do it continuously, not putting effort into your breath. Let it be effortless but deep.

Repeat this cycle twenty times, and you'll feel calmer. The brain switches from beta waves (when you're awake and engaged) to theta waves (relates to the subconscious mind). In theta waves, your brain interacts with different regions that aren't reachable when you're awake.

That's how you find answers.

It's a practice that should be performed every week. Know this: You won't change your life in one session. You'll learn to watch your thoughts and not judge or react. Just watch, realize, assess, fix, and elevate.

It's where you reflect on your mistakes, on the ego "I" self, and start living consciously.

Do it for yourself. Become better, and the world will become better.

■ ■ ■

Back to the Thursday I was talking about earlier. A few moments passed as I meditated. I was in stillness in an elevated state. I rewatched my run last year. It was as if all my running flashed in my head over a few seconds, and then a big realization slapped me in the face.

Before July 24, 2022, my first marathon barefoot, I was pushing to become better. It took me three years of effort, failures, and trials to get where I was.

It required daily effort from me, battling between the old self—the one who was only chasing pleasurable things and chasing his ego, fighting through the layers of doubts, fears, and confusion—and the true self who wanted to improve.

The books, the meditation, the runs, the promises, and the consistency behind the oath. These challenges were the daily wins I had to go through to be one percent better every day. After three years of pushing myself beyond what I thought was possible, I'm here today.

After paying all my debts, running toward my better self, dealing with all the layers, and becoming the person I always ought to be, I'm here today.

When I accomplished my first barefoot marathon on July 24, I was crying at the finish line because I was at the funeral of my old self, who I'd left under the tent. I was in tears because I let it go—I let go of fears, I let go of doubts, and I let go of my ego. I let go of the people, the pleasured me, the worried me, and the sick me.

Trust me, it's not easy to let go, especially of an identity I'd lived in for the past thirty years. But I buried my old self under the tent. I was touched by life on that day, and life will never be the same.

As soon as I had these realizations, a fire went through my body. A tear of happiness rolled down my face. I felt love. Love of oneself. Love of accepting myself, with my flaws, my past, and my mistakes, and gratefulness for being alive. I felt love a year ago, and since that day, I've been feeling it every day. It changed me.

Loving oneself doesn't mean to love the "I". It's beyond me. It's the love of everyone and everything. It's not a love of attachment or possession. It's actually a love of giving and appreciating.

Love life. Look around now while you're reading this book. You can breathe, you can think, and you can feel. You have a roof over your head and food on your plate. You're blessed, my friend.

Smile and be grateful because you are f**king alive. You have options. Don't ever let your mind (the devil) steal life from you. Push and keep pushing, face your fears, be uncomfortable, and give from your heart. Life is outside your mind.

I accepted what life offered me through the years—the good and the bad. I'm grateful for both. I'm a being beyond my name, beyond my nationality, and beyond my title. I'm like everything else. I'm passing through on a journey called life.

All my growth happened when I kept pushing beyond my mind. Picture this: an alarm goes off in your mind, and a war breaks out between "snooze it" versus "not today" versus "you can't do it" versus "let me try" versus "you're not good enough" versus "I'm fine not being good enough". The war between myself and the evil mind is a constant battle. No days off, believe me.

As Paramahansa Yogananda said, "He who conquers the mind conquers the world."

I'm ready for life, man, whatever it has in store for me. I know exactly what I want from life, and I'm going after it with no fear. I'll keep pushing myself. I'll go places that I personally thought were impossible. I'll keep sharing love with everyone and everything. I'll keep showing the world that love is the way. Love the effort, love the sweat, love the hardships, and love the failures, and you'll rise above them. You'll rise above your pain.

Love others, smile at others, and help others, even when your mind is convincing you not to. Push beyond your mind, and you'll become a better human. There's no easy way, and there are no shortcuts.

As my auntie kept saying, even until her last breath, "Love life."

Love it … Love it with all there is. Cry when you need to, then rise and try again. We're lucky to experience this dimension as humans. Do you know how good it is to be human?

It is f**king amazing to be a human, to be good, to do good, and to feel good.

Let's Live, baby! Every f**king day! Woohoo!

THERE IS NO REALITY

"We are creating realities with our own imagination."

— Walt Disney

At the beginning of 2023, I posted a video on all my platforms expressing my true thoughts.

"Mom still doubts that I will achieve my dreams" (this video was posted six months after the barefoot marathon). Yes, Mom loved me and supported me, but she still doubted where I was heading with my life.

"So, this year, I'm going to stop everything else. I'm going to take a loan (which I did from a friend), and I'm going to go all in on my dreams."

These were my goals:

1. Break a world record for a cause, which was achieved with the nail board.
2. Run over 1,000 kilometers, and I reached over 2,000 kilometers that year.
3. Write my book (which you're reading), and it will be published at the beginning of 2024.
4. Create quality content every day on social media. Quality content, as in one YouTube video a week. This goal will keep pushing me to learn and expand every day.
5. Meet Sadhguru.
6. Be on Joe Rogan's podcast.

I love Sadhguru and his wisdom and his perspective on life. He's a cool guru, and his wisdom and perspective on life initially ignited me. He approaches life in a way that allows us to understand our behavior and how our mind acts. For him, wisdom is the ultimate key.

I posted this video of my goals at the beginning of January 2023, and it got over one million views—a lot of support.

But remember, I had no idea how I'd meet Sadhguru or *if* I'd meet him. My intentions were pure, and I was working every day to be the best me. So, I decided to send him a DM every day throughout 2023, asking him (or probably his team handling social media) how I could meet him that year.

Days went by, and then weeks and months. In December 2023, I saw an advertisement for Sadhguru's upcoming visit to Dubai on December 9.

First, I was seriously mesmerized by life (God, Universe ... Whatever you like to call it)! During the last month of the year, Sadhguru was going to be in Dubai, and I knew deep within that I'd meet him (with pure honesty). After sending the intention and working baby steps toward it, it felt right somehow.

It was time to make it a reality. I felt it, man. I saw him and felt him in my meditations and my runs.

You're probably wondering how I felt him or saw him ... Let me explain before you become skeptical. Have an open mind and read on.

When running long distances, after ten kilometers, running turns into meditation; I enter a trance, an elevated state. My mind shuts down. I shift to my heart, and I'm in a loving state. I see my emotions and thoughts, yet I become detached from them.

My body is running on its own accord, and "the inner me" (my true self) is observing everything happening. In this state where life happens, I saw the image of meeting Sadhguru when he was in Dubai. I felt him the same way as when you think about someone, you love and feel them. I knew it was coming my way. I was in an elevated state, ready to receive.

I actually have a video that I filmed for myself. It was December 5, and I hadn't met Sadhguru yet. I met him "pointing at my heart" with tears in my eyes.

It's okay if what you read seems strange to you. I want to open the thought for you. I want you to be curious and look deep into what I said. No one taught me what I mentioned above, but I read many books talking about this concept. Finally, I understood and experienced it myself.

You can also reach it, though it's not easy, and it won't happen in a day. With constant effort, research, and experimentation, you'll get there.

A motto I also live by is, "Have a goal. Don't worry about the how. Think about the what, and it will manifest if you deserve it."

The first thing I did was buy a ticket to his event on December 9. Maybe I could have a conversation with him after the event. That wasn't all.

Second, I posted a video on my social media on November 29, sharing what I said in this chapter: "All the goals I aimed to achieve were complete, but this goal is out of my hands. If you believe I deserve to meet him, tag him, and send him this video as a DM."

Man, the love of people was beautiful; his team was bombarded with tags and DMs.

I heard the team received my request, but no one had contacted me yet.

Opportunities are like waves; they keep coming, but it's your job to catch the wave. Though some waves only come once in a while, I wasn't going to stand still waiting,

I'd use all the resources I had at that moment (my videos).

I also needed to keep trying, so on December 1, I posted another video, "Update about meeting Sadhguru: There are no updates yet." On December 3, another video, "Why do I want to meet Sadhguru?" I was putting all my thoughts and my intentions out there.

Still no reply. Nothing.

The last video I posted was on December 7. I was very clear and straightforward with what I wanted to say. "I'm Ramy Naouss, and I want to meet Sadhguru for twenty minutes to have a talk and add value to my community."

Definite aim, consistency, being ready and patient.

The same day, Kris Fade from Virgin Radio reached out to me. He said, "Hey Ramy, I saw you run barefoot. I'd love to have you on my morning show to talk about the run. Would you be keen to join us on Friday, December 9, at 8:00 a.m.?"

I replied, "Sure."

I woke up at 5:30 a.m., hit an ice bath, and ran to Virgin Radio's office. It was eight kilometers away—an easy run. As soon as I arrived, I changed my sportswear and dressed like a normal human being, cooling down while waiting my turn.

I was walking toward the studio, and as soon as I reached the door, I saw Sadhguru. I had zero expectations. Kris Fade from Virgin Radio, me, and Sadhguru. My mind really didn't connect the dots.

I'll be completely honest. I was in shock. Not only had I met Sadhguru, but the way it all manifested, everything I'd imagined was in front of me. It was all a reality at that moment.

I was like, "Wow!" in awe of life. Goosebumps. A rush of emotion. My body was electrified.

We had a nice conversation. We had around fifteen to twenty minutes on air, and it took me a good fifteen minutes to grasp everything that had happened.

I remember Kris asked Sadhguru for a few last words before we wrapped up the episode. Sadhguru started talking. I was seated to his right with my head tilted slightly toward the right, and I wasn't listening to what he was saying. I was taking mental pictures. Tears filled my eyes—how life is beautiful and has no limits, and how I was grateful to create a reality from my imagination.

I left the studio and went on my run back home high on life like every f**king day, with another memory stuck in the depths of my soul.

LET'S LIVE

> "It is not about adding days to your life,
> but it is about adding life to your days."

Here's how I changed my life drastically and how I'm living the life I always dreamed of. It's the end of 2023 at the time of writing this book. One goal wasn't achieved this year, and that was my goal to be on Joe Rogan's podcast. I know I'll be there eventually, but 2023 may not be the right time for it. So, I'm carrying this thought with me to 2024.

During these last twelve months, I lived more than I've lived during the previous thirty years. You can understand why after reading this book. I achieved all my goals in 2023 because they had been cooking away since January 2020.

I achieved them through definite aim, consistency, and patience.

Maybe it's not running barefoot or standing on nails for you, bro. Life has endless possibilities. Challenging yourself is the way.

Travel solo to a new country (the first trip I did solo took me to another mental level), fast for twenty-four hours, go to a monastery for a week, go on a retreat, lose weight, climb Mount Everest, do an ice bath, change how you dress for two weeks, leave your job or just change your job (only if you don't like it), start your business, learn how to paint, learn a new language, volunteer for a month, go camping in the forest for three days, cycle around Africa (my friend Roberto Helou is doing it this year—crazy!), run a marathon with or without shoes, or learn sky diving. Who cares?

Stretch yourself. Push yourself beyond your mind.

Start with whatever you can today; start by making your bed and take it from there.

You can do whatever you want, feel however you want and live however you f**king want.

Life begins with you and ends with you.

Only your mind will try to stop you, so push beyond the mind, and life will happen to you. Being scared, afraid, confused, worried, and sad is okay. Actually, it's okay to feel any emotion, but it's not okay not to live. You shouldn't be worried about dying. You should be worried about not living.

Answer this question:

There's a big room with a box in the middle, and all the people you love or care about are in this room. You walk into the room, but no one can see you. You're invisible because your body is in the box in the middle. Yes, it's in the coffin. You're dead, but you can hear and feel everyone.

What do you want them to say about you?

When I did this exercise, it hit me hard, man.

So, while you're alive, work for it because the most beautiful thing that happened to you and me is life itself.

Let's Live, baby, every f**king day. Woohoo!

CONCLUSION

I love you for taking the time and effort to read my book.

I genuinely love and appreciate you because I admire people trying, learning, searching, and developing themselves daily. I also hope one day we'll meet, and you'll share your story, challenges, and how you rose above your struggles, how you changed, or just any f**king thing you'd like to share with me.

I hope this book will inspire you to push yourself, tap into yourself, connect with yourself, and become more.

You're not a tree. You can change. It's possible. Take time to embrace the change. Live a conscious life, be aware of your actions, understand yourself, and you'll understand the world.

Keep in mind the devil within will keep on trying to steal life from you, but life will only happen beyond the mind.

Success isn't money in the bank. It's not having an expensive car, it's not followers on social platforms, and it's definitely not a title.

Having a lot of money isn't bad, but it *is* bad to be greedy for money. It isn't bad to drive the car you desire, except when you're doing it because your life is miserable and you're seeking approval from the world. It's amazing to have influence on social platforms and to use it for the betterment of the world. It isn't bad to have titles, but don't become the title.

Success is who you become, not in the eyes of society, but in your eyes. The ultimate success is going to bed smiling, feeling peace, and being proud of yourself.

Success is letting go of all that doesn't serve you. Let go of negative people you love if they pull you back. Let go of bad habits. Let go of negative thinking. Let it go.

Once you elevate as a human, become aware, and live consciously, life turns out to be bliss. There will always be challenges, but feeling at home is the ultimate peace. The rest will flow easily into your life. When you're home, your life will be filled with beautiful people, amazing experiences, infinite money, and endless love.

I was self-centered and selfish; I only cared about myself, was sick with cancer, and was broke. I then took control of my life, elevated as a human, and became a loving awareness, doing good, being good, and enjoying life.

I'll leave you with this:

It's easy to make a decision to change. It's easy to sit in silence in the morning for five minutes. It's easy to stop checking your phone as soon as you wake up. It's easy to push yourself. It's easy to try and become better.

But do you know what is also easy?

It's easy not to do it. It's easy to find an excuse. It's easy to do what everyone else is doing. It's easy to remain the same.

It's up to you to pick which type of easy you want in this life.

Get hungry for life, bro. Be great and live.

Let's Live, baby, every f**king day! Woohoo!

AUTHOR BIO

I'm Ramy Naouss.

I was diagnosed with cancer on January 8, 2017. I lost the meaning of life and felt confused and depressed.

After that day, I decided to get better through daily changes and small habits, such as reading, writing, meditating, running, and stepping out of my comfort zone.

I started growing. In 2022, I ran my first marathon barefoot. Something within me clicked. I learned that challenging myself is the way. I started running longer, all barefoot. I was taking myself within, isolating myself, and tapping into my true self.

In 2023, I listed some goals and achieved all of them. One of them was to set a world record for my auntie, who passed away from cancer.

On March 5, 2023, I set a world record for standing on nails for the longest duration. I did it for twelve hours, twelve minutes, and twelve seconds.

Since 2023, I've run around seven marathons and three ultramarathons barefoot. I've conducted events to share the concept of *Let's Live* in Lebanon and Dubai for more than 1,000 people.

I met Sadhguru and wrote my book.

And all this is just the beginning.

BLURB

Since 2022, Ramy Naouss and his motto, "Let's Live," have catapulted onto the internet, sharing his challenges, mindset, and approach to living a good life and—as he says—feeling alive. Through his book *Let's Live*, he shares his secrets, all his ways of self-reflection, and the effort and realization it took him to reach a high mental, physical, and spiritual state.

In this eye-opening memoir, author Ramy Naouss shows how making small changes on a daily basis can lead to big, meaningful changes in your life.

In *Let's Live*, Ramy Naouss talks about his inspirational journey, starting from living unhealthily, engaging in endless drinking and partying, and being diagnosed with cancer at an early age, then making the decision to change completely and live life to the fullest.

Ramy swears that the only way is to challenge yourself with daily small challenges to reach the inner power hidden within. He also loves reminding the world how powerful it is to be a human, to be good, and to feel good.

He believes you can accomplish the impossible when you find your inner power. He's proving it by achieving big challenges like running long distances barefoot, setting a world record standing on a nail board, and making big dreams his reality.

Notes

www.ingramcontent.com/pod-product-compliance
Lightning Source LLC
Chambersburg PA
CBHW030549080526
44585CB00012B/312